"It has been said that, of all the Christian gifts and virtues, the most difficult one to fake is assurance. In this book, Dr. Lawson makes clear that either you have it or you don't. He then proceeds, in clear, deliberate methodology, to lead the Christian who may have doubts to examine the biblical foundations upon which a lasting sense of security rests—convincing the insecure that 'if God be for us, who can be against us?' Good reading for all of us."

D. JAMES KENNEDY, PH.D.
FOUNDER OF EVANGELISM EXPLOSION
SENIOR MINISTER, CORAL RIDGE PRESBYTERIAN CHURCH
FORT LAUDERDALE, FLORIDA

"Steve Lawson writes with a pastor's heart and a passion for truth. *Absolutely Sure* is a wonderful and much-needed reminder that God intends for us to be certain of our salvation. Through reading this book, Christians will gain renewed confidence. Those uncertain of their salvation will come face to face with the power of the authentic gospel. We all stand in Steve Lawson's debt for this book which so clearly lays out God's purpose in our salvation."

DR. ALBERT MOHLER, JR.
PRESIDENT, SOUTHERN BAPTIST THEOLOGICAL SEMINARY
LOUISVILLE, KENTUCKY

"During a time in which so many are discarding absolute truth and accepting all pathways to heaven, it is now vital to send a clear and confident signal of God's salvation in Jesus Christ. Knowing what it means to be a genuine believer and to live in the absolute assurance of eternal salvation is critical to our spiritual well-being. Dr. Steve Lawson is one of the premier Bible expositors in our generation. He asks and answers the right questions and does it in a style that is sensible and applicable. I recommend this book highly to all who desire to be absolutely sure."

DR. JACK GRAHAM
SENIOR PASTOR, PRESTONWOOD BAPTIST CHURCH
DALLAS, TEXAS

"Steve Lawson writes with authority. This book is a sure path to dynamic certitude about the most important issue of life. His words penetrate like graced arrows."

DR. R. KENT HUGHES
SENIOR PASTOR, COLLEGE CHURCH
WHEATON, ILLINOIS

"In a day when so much of our theological thinking is dominated by postmodernism, it is refreshing to pick up a book with the title *Absolutely Sure!* The author, Steven Lawson, has settled the issue of eternal life in Christ by expounding the essential message of 1 John with its glorious affirmation that to believe in the name of the Son of God is to *know* that we have eternal life. Such assurance is based on the objective truth of God's inerrant Word. As Luther says in his *Large Catechism,* 'God does not lie. My neighbor and I—in short, all men—may err and deceive, but God's Word cannot err.' My friend, Steven Lawson has done a superb job and I commend his book with prayerful confidence."

DR. STEPHEN F. OLFORD
FOUNDER AND SENIOR LECTURER,
THE STEPHEN OLFORD CENTER FOR BIBLICAL PREACHING
MEMPHIS, TENNESSEE

*Settle the Question
of Eternal Life*

Absolutely

SURE

STEVEN J. LAWSON

Multnomah®Publishers *Sisters, Oregon*

ABSOLUTELY SURE
published by Multnomah Publishers, Inc.

and in association with the literary agency of Yates & Greer, LLP

© 1999 by Steven J. Lawson
International Standard Book Number: 1-57673-409-9

Front and back cover illustration by John Lund/Tony Stone Images
Design by Kirk DouPonce

Scripture quotations are from:
New American Standard Bible
© 1960, 1962, 1963, 1968, 1971, 1973, 1975, 1977, 1995
by the Lockman Foundation.
Used by permission.

Multnomah is a trademark of Multnomah Publishers, Inc.,
and is registered in the U.S. Patent and Trademark Office.
The colophon is a trademark of Multnomah Publishers, Inc.
Printed in the United States of America

For information:
MULTNOMAH PUBLISHERS, INC.
POST OFFICE BOX 1720
SISTERS, OREGON 97759

Library of Congress Cataloging-in-Publication Data:
Lawson, Steven J.
    Absolutely sure/by Steven J. Lawson.
        p.   cm.
    ISBN 1-57673-409-9 (alk. paper)
    1. Assurance (Theology)   2. Salvation   I. Title.
BT785.L38   1999
234—dc21   99-12145
                                                           CIP

99 00 01 02 03 04 — 10 9 8 7 6 5 4 3 2 1

This book is dedicated to
the precious people of

DAUPHIN WAY BAPTIST CHURCH

Especially to
Bill Arthur, Ed Ahrens,
and John Davis
and
our Deacon fellowship

whose unwavering commitment
to Christ has been
mightily used by God to build up
and extend His kingdom,

and most of all to

Bill Ladner
and
the Monday Morning
Men's Prayer Group

whose spiritual maturity
and intercessory prayers have upheld
and undergirded the ministries of our beloved church.

CONTENTS

FOREWORD

No one can be a victorious Christian or mighty in service to our Lord who does not have a "blessed assurance" of his or her salvation. Steve Lawson is a gifted communicator who has soaked himself in the Word of God. He sounds a certain and solid note in a discordant chorus of confusion. Many Christians are not walking in victory and are ineffective in their Christian service because of doubt. A wise man once said that serving God with doubt in your mind is like driving an automobile with the brakes on.

I have found that those who have a solid assurance of their salvation are the happiest and the healthiest Christians. The reason for this is simple—when we know the future is secure, we can then concentrate on the present.

And what does it take to give this assurance? It takes more than conjecture, emotionalism, or good intentions. We need the solid word that is in this wonderful book.

I expect at least five categories of readers to be enriched by this volume.

First of all, those who have a full and blessed assurance of their salvation will find cause again and again to rejoice in God's mighty mercies and fathomable grace.

Second, those who are saved but are living in doubt will be able to bring things into sharp focus and have the legacy that belongs to every child of God.

Third, pastors and preachers (that includes me) will find rich material to share with congregations. Preachers need all the help they can get, and we are often encouraged and instructed by the writing and preaching of others. I expect many grateful pastors will bless God for this book.

Next, I believe that Sunday school teachers will be blessed and instructed. This book would make a wonderful series of lessons. Every member of the class could be given a book or encouraged to buy one. Every class could be greatly strengthened.

Finally, it is my prayer that some who do not yet know Jesus Christ as personal Lord and Savior will read this volume and see how wonderful and blessed it is to trust in Jesus. It is my prayer that they will find that this salvation is simply glorious and gloriously simple.

Dear reader, get ready for a blessing!

Adrian Rogers, Pastor
Bellevue Baptist Church
Memphis, Tennessee

FOREWORD

Assurance of salvation. Complete certainty unassailed by anxiety and doubt. Is it possible? How may we *know* we are truly saved? I know of no single doctrinal issue that confuses people more than this one.

People who misconstrue the biblical doctrine of assurance tend to run to one or the other of two opposite extremes. On one hand, there are many who arrogate for themselves a false confidence. Having learned that salvation is a gift of divine grace, they falsely conclude that self-examination is therefore wholly unnecessary. Spiritual fruit? They regard it as optional and irrelevant to the matter of assurance. Their lives may be utterly devoid of any practical evidence of a vital union with Christ, but their smug self-confidence remains untroubled by that.

On the other hand, there are many who beat themselves up with constant anxieties and self-accusations, always looking for reasons to doubt rather than enjoy their standing in Christ. They seem morbidly obsessed with their failures, sinking into despair over every sign of fleshly deficiency they uncover in their hearts. And of course, the more they look within, the more their doubts increase.

Both groups have a tendency to hearken to instruction meant for the other. I've noticed over the years that when the stress is on biblical truths that expose and attack the false hopes of the overconfident, those who are overanxious invariably latch on to those warnings and use them to trouble themselves further. But when the emphasis is on matters such as justification by faith, the vastness of God's mercy, or the perfect freeness of God's saving grace, the overconfident feed their false assurance with comforts intended for others. Virtually every aspect of the biblical doctrine of assurance is therefore prone to being misunderstood and twisted. It is a difficult subject, filled with potential pitfalls.

That's why I'm grateful for Steve Lawson's latest book, *Absolutely Sure*. It is a lucid survey of the biblical doctrine of assurance from 1 John, perhaps the key passage on assurance in all of Scripture. In careful, clear, biblical fashion, Dr. Lawson outlines nine vital signs of assurance from this key passage of Scripture. He examines Christian assurance from all angles. No facet is left unexplored. No point is left imbalanced. He shows clearly how Scripture corrects both the chronic uncertainty of the overanxious and the superficial security of the overconfident.

Full assurance is the birthright of every genuine believer in Christ. No single doctrine in all of Scripture is more vital to the Christian's daily life than this one. A true, settled assurance is the necessary taproot by which all other spiritual fruit is nourished to health and maturity. No wonder this doctrine is the focus of so many attacks from the powers of darkness.

The pure light of Scripture is the only antidote to confusion and uncertainty on this and every other spiritual matter. Steve Lawson does a skillful job of focusing that light where it is most needed. The result is a book that will prove a valuable resource and a rich blessing to new believers and mature Christians alike. If you are struggling with assurance—or if you know someone else who is—I know you'll find in the pages that follow a rich wealth of spiritual treasure.

John MacArthur

ACKNOWLEDGMENTS

I want to express my gratitude to the people at Multnomah who have done so much to get this book into your hands, especially Rod Morris, my editor, who has patiently and skillfully worked with me.

I am deeply thankful for Jason Allen, who has helped review this manuscript, and Julie Riley, who has typed it.

I am very appreciative to Lance Quinn, who made many insightful recommendations to this project.

Most of all, I want to thank my family who has encouraged and prayed for me, especially my wife Anne, without whom my life and ministry would be so lacking.

INTRODUCTION

On a recent flight to Portland, Oregon, for a meeting with my publisher to finalize this book, I was seated next to a woman who, after a long period of silence, broke the ice by asking me where I was going.

"Sisters, Oregon," I replied. "Do you know where it is?"

"Oh, yes," she answered, explaining to me various routes through the mountains to get there. Then she cautioned me, "I've heard there's snow on the mountain passes leading to Sisters. You'd better get chains or snow tires for your rental car."

After I thanked her for her advice, she asked, "What's your business in Sisters?"

"I write books," I explained, "and I'm going to meet with Multnomah Publishers about my latest book."

"What kind of books?"

"Christian books."

"Really? What's this one about?"

"It's a book about how to be absolutely sure that you're going to heaven."

I'll never forget her response.

"Wow!" she blurted out, loud enough for all to hear. "You can know you're going to heaven?"

Realizing that God had opened a door for me to share Christ with her, I replied, "We can be absolutely sure about our eternal destiny. We can afford to be wrong about going to Sisters, Oregon, but we cannot afford to be wrong about going to heaven."

I then had the privilege of sharing with her, as well as with her traveling companion, the greatest truth anyone could ever tell another person—the gospel of Jesus Christ. I went on to say that not only can we possess eternal life now, but we can know that we have received it before we go to heaven.

I want you to know we can be sure we are going to heaven long before we arrive. Fact is, we can be just as certain that we are going to heaven as if we had already been there ten thousand years.

We live in a world that is constantly changing. The only thing constant, it has been said, is change. Certainty about anything these days is a rare commodity. We are becoming less and less sure about more and more issues. Who knows what tomorrow holds?

But in the midst of this world of uncertainty, we may have a confident hope for the future. We can be absolutely sure about our salvation in Jesus Christ. We can know with certainty that heaven is our final destination. We can know beyond a shadow of any doubt that eternal life is ours, long before we step into eternity.

Sound too good to be true? Perhaps—but it is true. God not only wants you to spend all eternity with Him, He desires you to be absolutely sure about it now.

The purpose of this book is to lay before you the biblical basis for the assurance of your salvation. In the pages that follow, we will examine how anyone who puts his trust in Jesus Christ can know with absolute certainty that he is saved and heaven-bound.

If you would like to settle the matter of eternal life, this book is for you. I don't believe anything happens by accident. There is a divine purpose and overriding plan for everything. There is a reason you are holding this book in your hands, and for many of you, it may well be God's means of helping you settle your eternal destiny. So come along with me as we look at God's Word together for solid, biblical answers to life's most important questions: "Am I saved or lost?" and "How can I know that I have eternal life?"

You can afford to be uncertain about some things in life, like going to Sisters, Oregon. But not about going to heaven.

For that, you need to be absolutely sure.

Chapter one

AIRTIGHT ASSURANCE

Saved and Sure!

1 JOHN 5:13

We prize full assurance beyond all price.
We count it to be a gem beyond all earthly values.

Charles H. Spurgeon

The year was 1912, and all of Britain was buzzing with talk of the R.M.S. *Titanic,* the largest ship ever built. She stretched three football fields in length, reached eleven stories in height, and weighed 46,000 tons. The crown jewel of Britain's White Star Line, the *Titanic* was the most impressive ocean liner to sail the seas—the largest moving object ever created. She was billed as the eighth wonder of the world. A veritable floating palace of staggering proportions, she was said to be the "unsinkable ship."

But tragically, sink is all she ever did.

On her fateful maiden voyage, the *Titanic* left Southampton, England, on April 12, 1912, carrying 1,312 passengers plus a crew and service staff of 914, heading for New York. As she crossed the North Atlantic, the *Titanic* received a warning at 9:40 P.M. on April 14 about "much heavy pack ice and great number of large icebergs." But wireless operator Jack Phillips placed the warning underneath a paperweight and continued sending personal messages for passengers.

Five more warnings were received—and five more warnings were discarded, the last one because no one wanted to awaken the captain.

Why should he be disturbed? After all, no one believed the ship could ever go down.

But at 11:40 P.M., Frederick Fleet, sitting lookout in the crow's nest, spotted an iceberg five hundred yards away and called the bridge. But it was too late. The *Titanic* struck a skyscraper-sized iceberg, ripping a fifteen-foot gash along the proud vessel's right side, resulting in the flooding of six of her sixteen watertight compartments.

At 12:45, the first lifeboat was lowered into the chilly waters below—half empty. Others tried to seek safety, but for most it was too late. Some jumped into the water and tried to swim, but hypothermia set in and they sank into a watery grave. Others stayed on board the ship, climbing to the highest point, but they also drowned in the chilly Atlantic. A few even went back to their cabins to grab their valuables, and they too drowned.

ONLY A FEW SAVED

In all, only 753 lives were saved. The few who believed and acted upon what others initially refused to accept, namely that the ship had struck an iceberg and was sinking, got into the lifeboats and were saved.

Having heard the frantic distress call of the *Titanic,* another ship, the *Carpathia,* arrived on the scene in less than an hour. The survivors were fished out of lifeboats and brought on board.

When news was telegraphed ahead to New York City, thousands of people gathered outside the White Star Shipping Line office to await the grim news. Who had been rescued? Who had perished?

On that day, it mattered not whether one had first-, second-, or third-class accommodations. It mattered not if one had been sailing on the starboard side or the port side. It mattered not if one had been the captain of the ship or merely a crew member.

When they posted the report next to each name, all that mattered was *saved* or *lost.*

WILL YOU BE SAVED?

This tragedy of yesteryear serves as a grim reminder of a far greater truth. Like the *Titanic,* this world is sailing proudly full speed ahead, ignoring constant warnings from heaven. Already she has struck the massive iceberg of sin—a grim reality many choose to deny—and is rapidly taking on the icy waters of God's judgment. This world is sinking and threatens to take down all on board.

There is only one hope of escaping eternal death and separation from God. That is to respond to God's warning now and come to faith in Jesus Christ. God offers salvation in His Son, but we must believe in Him and get into the lifeboat that alone will save us.

Will we heed God's warning? Will we get into the lifeboat of Christ's salvation? Or will we deny the warnings and go down with the ship?

THE GREATEST THING

The greatest thing in all the world is to be saved. The second is closely related. It is to be absolutely sure that you are saved.

People everywhere are wrestling with the issue of the assurance of their salvation. They want to know, Am I saved? Am I truly forgiven and right with God? When I die, will I go to heaven? Can I be sure? Upon what basis am I sure? How can I know that I'm born again?

These heart-searching questions reflect the concern of so many. With many fears and tears they search their souls, desperately seeking to know where they stand with God.

Am I saved, or am I lost?

Have you asked yourself this question recently? When you are alone and free to think, does this monumental issue surface in your heart? When you read your Bible, or when you sit in church, do you think about this? When you hear the gospel of Jesus Christ preached, does this question echo in your mind?

Am I saved or lost?

R E S O L V I N G   T H E   U N C E R T A I N T Y

Until this issue is resolved, your life will be perpetually unsettled, tossed back and forth like the pounding waves of the sea. It's hard, even impossible, to live for God today when you are uncertain about where you will spend your eternal tomorrow. How can you have confident direction for the present when your future is so unsure? Truth be known, you can't.

Does the Bible hold any help for you? Can God direct your heart to be absolutely sure where you stand with Him? Can you know that you have eternal life?

The answer to these questions is *yes*. We can know that we are going to heaven long before we go there. We can know for certain that salvation in Jesus Christ is our present possession. We can be absolutely sure!

The Bible promises that we may have a settled confidence that eternal life belongs to us now. Scripture says we can have the "full assurance of faith" (Hebrews 10:22) that we are bound for heaven. God's Word teaches that we can make certain we are saved (2 Peter 1:10).

A   B O O K   O F   A S S U R A N C E

One book in the Bible was written for the express purpose of addressing the assurance of our salvation. Under the inspiration of the Holy Spirit, the New Testament book of 1 John was included in the Scriptures with this need in mind.

With apostolic authority coupled with pastoral care, John wrote this book to assist you in discerning if you are truly a Christian. By this I do not mean a Christian in name only. Anyone can take the name of Christ and identify himself outwardly with the Lord Jesus, yet inwardly not be born again, just as anyone can buy a Dallas Cowboys sweatshirt or jersey and wear it in public, yet not be on the active roster of the Dallas Cowboys. Almost anyone can have the outward association if they so desire, but relatively few know the inward reality of actually being on the Lord's team.

The purpose of 1 John is to help you and me determine, under the guidance of the Holy Spirit, whether or not we are genuine children of God. Am I a true believer or merely a make-believer? Am I a contender or only a pretender?

THE KEY VERSE

The key verse of 1 John that explains this overarching purpose is found in the last chapter of the book.

> These things I have written to you who believe in the name of the Son of God, in order that you may know that you have eternal life. (1 John 5:13)

As the apostle writes, he does so with unmistakable purpose. His reason for writing is clear: one, to help those who already believe to gain the certainty of their salvation, and two, to expose those who are religious but lost and awaken them to their unsaved condition so that they may come to a true knowledge of Christ.

There are several key words or phrases in 1 John 5:13: *written, believe, Son of God, know,* and *eternal life.* Each of these plays a strategic role in unlocking the door that leads to the assurance of our salvation. Let's examine them one at a time.

A KNOW-SO SALVATION

The first key word of 1 John 5:13, as well as of this entire epistle, is *know.* John writes, "in order that you may know that you have eternal life." Unmistakably, God wants all true believers to have the firm assurance of their salvation. He does not say, "These things I have written to you who believe in the name of the Son of God, in order that you may hope, guess, speculate, or wish that you have eternal life."

Instead, God writes, "that you may know that you have eternal life." God wants you to be certain of your relationship to Him. He wants you to know—no ifs, ands, or buts about it—that, if you are a genuine believer in Christ, you have eternal life. More than a mere possibility, assurance is the promised privilege of every child of God, a divinely granted birthright that accompanies salvation.

First John is a book of Christian certainty written that we may be absolutely sure that we have eternal life. John writes:

- By this we *know* that we are in Him. (2:5)
- I have written to you, children, because you *know* the Father. (2:13)
- But you have an anointing from the Holy One, and you all *know*. (2:20)
- I have not written to you because you do not *know* the truth, but because you do *know* it. (2:21)
- We *know* that when He appears, we shall be like Him. (3:2)
- We *know* that we have passed out of death into life. (3:14)
- We shall *know* by this that we are of the truth. (3:19)
- And we *know* by this that He abides in us. (3:24)
- By this you *know* the Spirit of God. (4:4)
- By this we *know* that we abide in Him and He in us. (4:13)
- By this we *know* that we love the children of God. (5:2)
- We *know*...we *know*...we *know*. (5:18–20)

God wants us to know that we belong to Him. Eternal life is not an issue that He wants clouding our minds with doubt, but something He desires to be clear in our hearts. Without any equivocation, God wants us to have a "know-so" salvation. Figuratively speaking, He does not want you to be a question mark, all bent over in doubt with your head hung low. Rather, He wants you to be an exclamation mark, standing erect with head held high, strengthened by a God-produced confidence in your faith in Him.

C. H. Spurgeon, the great British preacher, said he was so sure of his salvation that he could grab onto a cornstalk, swing out over the fires of hell, look into the face of the devil, and sing, "Blessed assurance, Jesus is mine!"

This very assurance should grip our hearts as well.

HOW FIRM A FOUNDATION

The second key word in 1 John 5:13 is the word *written*. John says, "These things I have written to you...." With deliberate emphasis, the apostle states that the assurance of our salvation rests upon the impregnable rock of God's Word. Our confidence about heaven is based solely upon what God says in Scripture regarding the gospel of Jesus Christ. It is on this basis alone that we may be absolutely sure that we belong to Him.

Unfortunately, too many want to gauge where they stand with God by their feelings. But such a "goose bump" approach to matters of eternal life is subject to fluctuating mood swings, fragile personalities, and fickle temperaments. In addition, loss of sleep, pressure at work, home, or school, hormones, and physical problems can greatly affect one's feelings about their relationship with God.

Those who rely on feelings for the assurance of their salvation will be riding an emotional roller coaster. When they are up, they feel saved; when they are down, they feel lost.

I pity the person who attempts to live this way. Only the eternal unchanging Word of God can be the ultimate basis for our assurance. The Scriptures alone are the rock-solid foundation upon which full assurance is built.

In the early twentieth century, Harry A. Ironside was the pastor of Moody Memorial Church in downtown Chicago. An elderly man confessed to him desperate struggles with the assurance of his salvation. He told Ironside how he longed for some sign from heaven, or hoped for some unmistakable witness, that he was truly saved.

"Suppose you had a vision of an angel who told you your sins were forgiven," Ironside said. "Would that be enough to rest on?"

"Yes," the man replied, "I think it would. An angel should be right."

"But suppose on your deathbed Satan came and said, 'I was your angel.' What would you say?"

The man was speechless.

Ironside then told him that God has given us something far more reliable and authoritative than the voice of an angel. That sure witness is His Word. "Isn't that enough to rest on?" this noted pastor asked.

I believe God asks us the same. "Isn't that enough?"

The authority of Scripture is enough. It is sufficient to fortify our faith and give even the weakest saint the settled confidence of his or her salvation. Ultimately, the certainty that one possesses eternal life rests upon believing what God has said in His Word. As the great hymn says,

> How firm a foundation, ye saints of the Lord,
> Is laid for your faith in His excellent Word!
> What more can He say than to you He hath said—
> To you, who for refuge to Jesus have fled?

BELIEVING IN CHRIST

The third key word in 1 John 5:13 is *believe*: "These things I have written to you who believe in the name of the Son of God...." In order to have assurance, we must believe in Jesus Christ. What does it mean to believe? It means to respond with one's entire being to Christ—mind, emotion, and will. With my mind, I must know the essential truths of the gospel, namely that I am a great sinner, Christ is a great Savior, and I must put my trust in Him. With my emotions, I must be persuaded of the certainty of these facts, convinced of my need. And with my will, I must commit myself to Christ alone to save me. As an act of my will, I must turn from my sins and entrust myself to Him, no longer relying upon my good works to commend me toward God.

Saving faith is the abandonment of my life to Christ who died for me. It is a decisive turning from sin and trusting Him to save me. More than mere intellectual assent and emotional feelings, it is the choice of my will to receive Christ to be my personal Lord and Savior.

What if I trust in Christ *and* something else to save me? What if I look to Him and my baptism to get me to heaven? Or what if I depend upon Him and my church membership, or my morality, or my good works, to possess eternal life?

If that is the case, then I have not yet come all the way to Christ and fully believed in Him. If my trust is 90 percent in Christ and 10 percent in my religious activity, I have not yet put 100 percent of my faith in Christ. Saving faith is a complete trust in Christ alone to save me.

Only those who trust in Christ alone may be saved. And only those who trust in Him alone may have the assurance of their salvation.

ALL OR NOTHING

Picture a man at the airport. With ticket in hand, he checks in for his boarding pass and walks down the ramp to the door of the plane. He stands in the open door and places one foot in the plane while keeping one foot on the ramp.

At this point, he has not fully committed himself to the plane. As long as only one foot is on board the plane and the other remains on the ramp, he remains uncommitted. But I can assure you, when the plane pulls out, he will have to choose one way or the other. Not until both feet are in the cabin of the plane does he entrust himself to it.

So it is with faith in Christ. As long as I have one foot on Christ and one foot on my religious efforts—walking an aisle, being baptized, joining the church, doing good works—I have not yet come all the way to Christ. Not until I abandon all my self-efforts and put my entire trust in Christ alone have I truly believed in Him for salvation.

Anything less is not a genuine faith that saves.

There is a superficial faith that is not saving faith. John tells us that "many believed in His name.... But Jesus, on His part, was not entrusting Himself to them, for He knew all men" (John 2:23–24). They believed with a spurious faith, and Jesus knew it and chose not to commit Himself to them. Even the devil believes, but not with a commitment leading to salvation (James 2:19). Some of the strongest testimonies in Scripture about Christ come from demon spirits, but no one would suggest they were saved (Matthew 8:29; Mark 1:24; 5:7; Luke 4:34; 8:28). Only the faith that knows (mind), affirms (emotions), and commits (will) to the truth of the gospel is genuine saving faith leading to assurance.

MAKING A COMMITMENT

Has there ever been a time in your life when you have believed in Jesus Christ? Have you ever committed your life to Jesus Christ who died for you upon the cross?

Assurance of salvation begins by establishing that you have trusted Christ alone for salvation. Not relying upon your own goodness or religious activity, you have put your faith in Christ alone to save you. Affirming that you have taken such a decisive step of faith to come to Christ is absolutely necessary for assurance.

Have you confessed your sin and transferred your trust from yourself to Jesus Christ to save you? Have you ever entered by faith through the narrow gate that leads to life? Jesus said, "Unless one is born again, he cannot see the kingdom of God" (John 3:3).

CROSSING THE LINE

Some people can point to an exact time and specific place when they were converted to Christ. Others cannot. Instead, they can only look to a general period of time when they came to Christ, such as a week or month or season. Can this person have blessed assurance?

Absolutely! Think of it this way. Two travelers journey from Dallas,

Texas, to Little Rock, Arkansas. One is traveling by car, the other by plane.

When the one traveling by car crosses the Texas-Arkansas state line, he knows the exact moment he does so. A huge sign reads, Welcome to Arkansas. A visitor's center is positioned at the state line. An Arkansas state flag is flying.

But the one traveling by plane can only guess at the time when he crosses the state line. High above the clouds, he can barely make out the terrain below. He cannot read the welcome sign nor see the visitor's center. Instead, he can tell by the change in geography below—the increase in trees and the beginning of some wooded mountains—that he has left Texas and crossed over into Arkansas.

They both arrive safe and sound at their destination, but only one can recite the exact time he crossed the state line. The other can only refer to an approximate time. Yet they both have arrived safely at their destination.

ENTERING THE KINGDOM

The same is true in salvation. Some people, like the man driving the car, can point to an exact moment when they crossed the line and entered the kingdom of God. Because of the circumstances surrounding their conversion, passing from the state of being lost to the state of salvation was crystal clear. Many factors play a part in this—the clarity of the preacher, the age of the one being saved, the depth of the conviction of sin, the disciple-making that followed. All these are strategic if one is to point to the exact time he or she was saved.

The apostle Paul experienced this. He could take us to a specific place on the road to Damascus and tell us exactly where he was saved. When he gave his testimony later, he could pinpoint the time, the date, and the place.

But others, like the man who flew by plane, cannot identify the exact moment they crossed the line and departed from being lost to entering the kingdom of God. Instead, they can only look to an approximate period of time when God worked in their heart to bring about faith.

Are they any less saved? No. Should their assurance of salvation be any less? No. More important than when one began to believe in Christ is whether one believes in Him now. What is most critical is that one is a believer presently. What matters is that a person has crossed the line, leaving behind a life of sin, and has entered into eternal life.

Let me ask you: Do you believe in Jesus Christ as your Lord and Savior? I'm not asking you when did you, but do you this moment believe in Him? If so, then assurance can be yours.

Implicit in all true faith is assurance. Scripture says, "Now faith is the assurance of things hoped for, the conviction of things not seen" (Hebrews 11:1). An indispensable component of genuine, saving faith is the assurance of what is hoped for. That is to say, a confident assurance is inherent in genuine faith.

NAME ABOVE EVERY NAME

The fourth key in 1 John 5:13 is the phrase *Son of God*. The apostle writes to those "who believe in the name of the Son of God." Faith is no greater than its object, and Christ is its greatest object.

By "the name of the Son of God," John means all the essential truths of who Christ is and why He came, namely that Jesus is God come in human flesh to redeem us from our sins. To believe in His name means to trust completely in Christ to save you. Believing upon any other so-called Jesus would be eternal disaster. In 1 John, the apostle teaches that salvation is in His name alone.

- The blood of Jesus His Son cleanses us from all sin. (1:7)
- We have an Advocate with the Father, Jesus Christ the righteous, and He Himself is the propitiation for our sins. (2:1–2)

- He appeared in order to take away sins; and in Him there is no sin. (3:5)
- The Son of God appeared for this purpose, that He might destroy the works of the devil. (3:8)
- He laid down His life for us. (3:16)
- God has sent His only begotten Son into the world so that we might live through Him. (4:9)
- God loved us and sent His Son to be the propitiation for our sins. (4:10)
- This is the one who came by water and blood, Jesus Christ; not with the water only, but with the water and with the blood. (5:6)
- God has given us eternal life, and this life is in His Son. (5:11)
- Jesus Christ...is the true God and eternal life. (5:20)

Salvation comes as we rest in the finished work of Jesus Christ upon the cross—and so does assurance. Only as we understand that He accomplished all that is necessary for the forgiveness of our sins may we have the settled confidence of our salvation. If we assume, wrongly so, that we must achieve good works to maintain our right standing before God, then assurance will never be our possession. But as we trust the perfection of His saving death, then—and only then— may we enjoy a blessed assurance.

SAFE AND SURE FOREVER

I heard about two men who were on board a large ocean liner caught in the midst of a ferocious Atlantic storm. One man, who had never sailed before, was terrified that the ship was going down and he would perish.

He said to the other, "Aren't you scared? We may not make it!"

But his fellow companion, an experienced sailor of many voyages, replied, "This ship has been through far worse storms than this. Don't you worry, she's not about to go down."

Think about it. Both men were equally safe. They both sailed aboard the same ship. But only one had the assurance that they would safely arrive at their port of destination. The other man, though equally safe, feared for his life.

This reminds me of so many regarding their salvation in Jesus Christ. Many have believed in Christ, but not all fully understand that Christ will safely transport to heaven all who put their trust in Him. Jesus has never lost a one who has gotten on board with Him—and He never will.

Only when we understand the sufficiency of Christ's death and the fullness of His salvation can we enjoy with assurance the trip to heaven through the storms of life.

POSSESSING ETERNAL LIFE

The fifth key that we want to consider from 1 John 5:13 are the words *eternal life*. Vital to any true assurance is the understanding of what eternal life is. How can you be sure of your salvation if you are not quite sure what it is?

Salvation is, John says, possessing eternal life, which is, as its name implies, the very life of God in the human soul. It is the supernatural life of God invading the empty, dead soul of sinful man.

Essentially, eternal life is receiving a person, Jesus Christ. It is Christ Himself coming to live within us and giving to us the very life that He possesses. First John 5:20 says, "And we know that the Son of God has come, and has given us understanding so that we might know Him who is true; and we are in Him who is true, in His Son Jesus Christ. This is the true God and eternal life." In this verse, the apostle declares, Jesus is eternal life. To possess Christ is to possess eternal life because He is the eternal life (1 John 1:2).

Jesus said, "This is eternal life, that they may know You, the only true God, and Jesus Christ whom You have sent" (John 17:3). Eternal life is knowing God and Jesus Christ in a personal relationship by faith.

A NEW KIND OF LIFE

Eternal life is not primarily referring to a length of time. Everyone will live forever either in heaven or hell. So eternal life refers not so much to the duration of life, but to the quality of it.

It is Christ living in me that radically changes me. He takes up His royal residence in our once meaningless lives and gives to us abundant life (John 10:10). He fills us with the fullness of His presence, infusing us with all that accompanies divine life—the energy, growth, movement, and dynamic of God within us.

A LIFE-CHANGING REALITY

When the eternal life of Christ Himself lives within us, we are radically changed. There is no way we will continue to walk down the same old paths after receiving eternal life. No way!

Can I be a Christian and my life never change?

Impossible.

As we can see these changes within us, they bring us the blessed assurance that Christ lives in us and that salvation is real. I can know that I have truly believed in Christ as I see His life-changing power in my life.

So, what are the identifiable characteristics of eternal life? What changes should we look for in our life that, when we see them, bring the assurance of our salvation?

The book of 1 John records the clear evidences of eternal life in the one who has believed in Jesus Christ. Because the new birth infuses divine life into our once dead souls, it becomes obvious over time who has truly believed in Christ. As faith deepens, so the assurance of our salvation deepens as we see God's grace at work within us bringing about these changes. This is not a works salvation, but a salvation that works.

ETERNAL LIFE IS FOREVER

Moreover, eternal life goes on forever. As believers, our relationship with Christ will never end, not in this life nor in the life to come. If we could live for ten years and then lose our salvation, we would possess "ten-year" life. But we possess eternal life. What is settled for eternity cannot be undone in time.

Eternal life begins the moment we believe. "He who has the Son has the life; he who does not have the Son of God does not have the life" (1 John 5:12). The verbs *has* and *have* are in the present tense indicating that right now, presently, is when eternal life begins. It becomes ours the moment we believe in Christ.

Even death itself cannot stop eternal life. This life of God within us begins now when we believe and endures forever throughout all the ages to come. Jesus said, I am the resurrection and the life; he who believes in Me shall live even if he dies, and everyone who lives and believes in Me shall never die (John 11:25–26).

VITAL SIGNS OF SALVATION

Think of these evidences of eternal life as the vital signs a doctor looks for in a dying patient. If he wants to know if his patient is alive, he checks his vitals. A pulse, heart rate, breath, alert eyes, a response to pain—all these things reveal to a doctor that his patient has life. Without these vital signs, there can only be one conclusion: the patient is dead.

How can you know if you have eternal life? There are vital signs that you can check in your own life. If you receive a positive reading, you can know that you have eternal life pulsating through your soul. But an absence of these vital signs is cause for alarm.

The remainder of this book will carefully examine each of these vital signs to help you take the pulse of your spiritual life. Here's how you can take a "spiritual checkup" and determine whether or not you possess eternal life.

- Vital Sign #1: Communion with Christ (1 John 1:1–4)
- Vital Sign #2: Confession of sin (1 John 1:5–2:2)
- Vital Sign #3: Commitment to God's Word (1 John 2:3–6)
- Vital Sign #4: Compassion for believers (1 John 2:7–11; 3:14–18; 4:7–21)
- Vital Sign #5: Change of affection (1 John 2:12–17)
- Vital Sign #6: Comprehension of the truth (1 John 2:18–27; 4:1–6)
- Vital Sign #7: Conformity to Christlikeness (1 John 2:28–3:10)
- Vital Sign #8: Conflict with the world (1 John 3:11–13)
- Vital Sign #9: Confidence in prayer (1 John 3:19–24; 5:14–15)

All nine of these vital signs will be present in varying degrees in everyone who possesses eternal life. It is not that two or three of these vital signs will be present, nor five or six. All nine will be found in the one who truly believes in Jesus Christ.

Have you believed in Jesus Christ? Have you trusted Him alone to be your Savior and Lord? Receiving the assurance of our salvation is a clear-cut matter of reading your vitals. We can know that our faith is real as we see the evidence of a changed life.

But before we look at each of these vital signs that leads to the true assurance of salvation, we must first address another critical matter— exposing and tearing down false assurance.

Read on.

THE ULTIMATE DECEPTION

Religious but Lost

The road to hell often leads from the portals of heaven.

John Bunyan

hings aren't always what they appear to be. I never knew this to be more true than when I entered the ministry. Upon graduating from seminary, my first ministry assignment was working in a church with college students and young married couples. It was during that time that I made a startling discovery that has influenced me to this very day. To my amazement, many of the church members I served had lived many years under the false assurance of their salvation.

This sobering realization first hit me when I hosted an out-of-town weekend retreat for a group of young married couples. Some forty husbands and wives traveled with me to a beautiful Ozark Mountain chateau, an ideal place for solitude and reflection. That Friday night, as we gathered together in a large meeting room for our first session, I asked everyone to share how they came to know Jesus Christ. I was totally unprepared for what I heard.

Over half the group that evening gave essentially the same testimony. Again and again, they shared that years earlier they had gone to church, walked an aisle, talked with a counselor, prayed a prayer, been baptized, and presented to the church as a new Christian. But by their own sad admission, their life never changed. Despite this initial step toward Christ, they continued to live indifferently toward God, to run with the world, and to pursue sin with increasing pleasure.

By their own testimony, their lives never changed because they had not been born again. They had merely gone through the outward motions of a religious activity without experiencing the inward reality of regeneration. Not until some years later did they come to this sobering awareness. Only then did they realize that they were lost. And only then were they born again.

I was shocked. The majority of this group had grown up in Bible-believing churches but had lived their lives for many years under the deadly delusion that they were in God's kingdom. Although they had received the well-meaning assurance of a counselor, a pastor, or a parent, they had never received the true assurance of the Holy Spirit.

Think about it. Over half the people that weekend said they had been religious, but lost. I find that frightening! Even more alarming is the likelihood that this experience is but a microcosm of the church today. Vast multitudes within Christendom, I believe, profess to know Christ but by their deeds deny Him.

NOTHING HAS CHANGED

After two decades of pastoring and preaching around the country, it is my conviction that many professing Christians live under a false assurance of their salvation. Though they attend church and are out-wardly religious, many of them devoutly so, they nevertheless remain lost.

Following this first ministry assignment, I pastored another church for the next fourteen years and can say that most of those con-verted during that time were members of that church—fine, upstand-ing, seemingly moral people. They were Sunday school teachers, deacons' wives, choir members, and the like, people who had spent the majority of their lives under the delusion that they were Christians when they were not.

The same self-deception has been evident in the church I pastor presently. If we could pull back the veil and see what God sees, we would discover that this deadly illusion is but the tip of the iceberg for much of present-day Christendom.

THE GREATER DANGER

Worse than a genuine Christian who lacks the assurance of eternal life is the person who is lost but has a false assurance of his or her salvation. Despite this person's claim to know Christ, the counterfeit Christian remains lost in a world of deadly self-deception.

Of far greater danger than lacking the assurance of salvation is possessing a false assurance about a supposed salvation that is not real. This false assurance is the deadly delusion of thinking you are inside the kingdom of God when, in fact, you stand outside of it. Presuming you know Christ, in reality you merely know about Him. Thinking you see, you actually are blind. Believing you are going to heaven, you will awaken one day to the flames of hell, never to escape. This is the fatal delusion of being religious but lost.

EARLY DECEPTION

This deception was a real and present danger in John's day as he addressed the early church. In the first congregations were many who participated in the life of the church but had not participated in the life of Christ. Although actively involved, they were not personally converted. In the letter of 1 John, the apostle warns:

- If we say that we have fellowship with Him and yet walk in the darkness, we lie and do not practice the truth. (1:6)
- If we say that we have no sin, we are deceiving ourselves and the truth is not in us. (1:8)
- If we say that we have not sinned, we make Him a liar and His word is not in us. (1:10)

- The one who says, "I have come to know Him," and does not keep His commandments, is a liar, and the truth is not in him. (2:4)
- The one who hates his brother is in the darkness and walks in the darkness, and does not know where he is going because the darkness has blinded his eyes. (2:11)
- They went out from us, but they were not really of us; for if they had been of us, they would have remained with us; but they went out, so that it would be shown that they all are not of us. (2:19)
- Whoever denies the Son does not have the Father. (2:23)
- The one who practices sin is of the devil. (3:8)
- Everyone who hates his brother is a murderer; and you know that no murderer has eternal life abiding in him. (3:15)
- The one who does not love does not know God, for God is love. (4:8)
- If someone says, "I love God," and hates his brother, he is a liar; for the one who does not love his brother whom he has seen, cannot love God whom he has not seen. (4:20)

Every one of these verses describes one in the church who is religious but lost. Such intentional repetition by the apostle John underscores a significant danger that existed in the first century church—and is with us to this day. There are many who name the name of Christ but do not know Him.

DECEIVED AND DELUDED

According to these verses from 1 John, they claim to have fellowship with God and call other Christians their brother, but these people are sadly deceived. There is no confession of sin (1:6, 8, 10), no obedience to the Word (2:4), no love for the brethren (2:11, 3:15; 4:8, 20), no confession of Christ as Lord (2:23), and no practice of righteousness (3:8).

What are we to make of such confessing Christians? How are we to see their spiritual standing before God?

Lest there be any misunderstanding, no confession of sin or Christ, no obedience, love, or righteousness means no conversion, no salvation, and no heaven. The practice of their lives betrays the confession of their lips. Although they claim a relationship with Christ, it is nonexistent.

Tragically, the longer they go to church and are exposed to the truth without being converted, the harder their hearts become. Rather than softening their hearts to the work of the Holy Spirit, they resist Him and become callous, often unconsciously.

A DEADLY DOSE OF RELIGION

Here's how it works. A person goes to the doctor to get a tuberculosis shot so as not to contract the dreaded disease. The doctor, to prevent the patient from contracting the illness, actually injects him with a small dose of the virus itself. Strangely enough, a small dose of TB prevents one from contracting the full-blown disease. The shot serves to build up the patient's immunity to it. The lesser prevents the greater, keeping one from acquiring the real thing.

This is precisely what happens to so many people spiritually. They receive a small dose of religion, but it only inoculates them, preventing them from receiving the one true reality—Jesus Christ. They come to church, read their Bible, pray, even shed tears, but are never born again. Through increased exposure to Christ, their resistance to the convicting work of the Holy Spirit is built up, thus hardening their hearts and keeping them from entering into a personal relationship with Jesus Christ.

Untold multitudes of people within the church today are just like this. They have been inoculated with the gospel but never "contract" the real thing. They have walked an aisle, prayed a prayer, signed a card, made a decision, and been baptized. They have joined the church, attended Sunday school, sung in the choir, given their money, even served in church leadership. But despite all this, they have never been converted to Jesus Christ.

- They have facts about Christ but not faith in Him.
- They have believed with their head but not with their heart.
- They have come to church but not to Christ.
- They profess Christ but do not possess Him.
- They have turned over a new leaf but not received a new life.
- They have been reformed but not reborn.
- They wear a cross but never bear one.
- They know the Word of God but not the God of the Word.
- They give their money to God but not their life.
- They have practical religion but not a personal relationship with Christ.

SINCERE, BUT SINCERELY WRONG

So many talk about reaching the unchurched, and rightfully so, but our first mission field lies within the walls of the church itself. Truth be known, the unconverted church member is the hardest person to reach with the gospel. Assuming he is saved, he turns a deaf ear to the gospel, never applying it to his own life.

Such a person does not need assurance, but to have what assurance he does have, false as it is, stripped away. Before he can have a true assurance of salvation, he must wake up to his lost condition and be saved.

FEW FIND IT!

Behind all false assurance lies the deadening delusion of the great deceiver himself, Satan. This damning deception is nothing new. Jesus Himself warned it would be so. When speaking to the religious crowd of His day He said, "Not everyone who says to Me, 'Lord, Lord,' will enter the kingdom of heaven" (Matthew 7:21). In other words, many will profess to know Christ but in actuality do not.

Such self-deception is not for lack of religious activity or spiritual fervency. Of these who claim to know Christ, Jesus said, "Many will say to Me on that day, 'Lord, Lord, did we not prophesy in Your name, and in Your name cast out demons, and in Your name perform many miracles?'" (Matthew 7:22). Great numbers will be actively serving in the name of Christ yet still will not know Him.

On the final day, it will be to these counterfeit Christians that Jesus will say, "I never knew you; depart from Me, you who practice lawlessness" (Matthew 7:23). Many within Christendom—not a few—will profess to know Christ but will be rejected by Him in the final judgment. Presuming that they will be admitted into heaven, they will receive the shock of their lives when they are eternally banned from His presence and sentenced to hell forever.

Many profess to know Him, Jesus warned, but most do not. He instructed, "Enter through the narrow gate; for the gate is wide and the way is broad that leads to destruction, and there are many who enter through it. For the gate is small and the way is narrow that leads to life, and there are few who find it" (Matthew 7:13–14). Of those who claim allegiance to Him, many are on the broad path; only a few are on the narrow path. Did you hear that? *Many* are on the broad path; *few* are on the narrow.

The majority of those who say, "Lord, Lord" are traveling the broad path of religion that leads to eternal destruction. Most who prophesy, cast out demons, and perform miracles in Jesus' name do not know the One of whom they speak and serve. Only a few who claim to know Christ actually do. That is Jesus' appraisal and must be ours as well.

Churches everywhere are full of lost, religious people. From the pulpit to the pew, many have heads full of knowledge about Christ but hearts devoid of a personal relationship with Him. The message of the

Cross has never yet converted their lives. The gospel is always for someone else, they think, but never for them.

WHERE DO YOU STAND?

Some of you reading these pages actually know Christ but have lingering doubts about your salvation. Although you really are converted, you nevertheless find yourself still wondering, "Am I really a Christian?" In this book, I want to help you settle this in your heart. Our Lord desires that all true believers be absolutely sure about eternal life (1 John 5:13). If you have truly believed upon Christ and trusted Him to be your Lord and Savior, God wants you to know the assurance of your salvation.

But, on the other hand, others of you falsely assume that you are a Christian. You have lived for many years with the deadly delusion that you know Christ, when in reality you are one of "the many" who attend church and go through religious activities yet still travel the broad path headed to destruction. Maybe you have had a haunting suspicion that this could be true of you, but have suppressed it. I plead with you, don't be deceived. Scripture tells us all, "Test yourselves to see if you are in the faith; examine yourselves!" (2 Corinthians 13:5).

There is no greater portion of Scripture to test the genuineness of our faith than the book of 1 John. Written to help us determine whether or not our faith is real, this book provides the true basis by which we can conduct a sound, thorough spiritual inventory. Here is the divine standard we must apply if we are to discern whether our faith is a saving faith.

A WIN/WIN SITUATION

Whenever we put our faith under the microscope and examine its authenticity, it's always a win/win situation. Upon scrutinizing our faith in Christ, if we receive confirmation from God that our salvation is real, then that realization brings great peace and joy.

But if that same self-examination reveals that our faith is not authentic, that too is good. Only then do we understand that we are lost and see the need to be saved. So either way, whether the test reveals that we are saved, leading to assurance, or whether it reveals we are lost, leading to salvation, it is a win/win situation.

The only way for this to become a lose/lose situation is for us never to examine our faith. As one famous theologian noted, "The only life worth living is the examined life."

GOD AT WORK

As alarming as this deadly deception is within the church, I have been thrilled to see God perform extraordinary works of saving grace in the lives of many who had lived for many years under the delusion of a bogus faith. As they have sat under the sound preaching of the gospel, along with a clear explanation of the necessary evidences of salvation from 1 John, God has been pleased to open blind eyes, unstop deaf ears, and convict hardened hearts, leading to the conversion of many.

Witnessing these dramatic conversions has been one of the greatest joys of my life. To see God work in such a supernatural way, converting so many churchgoing people who were once deceived about their salvation, has greatly authenticated the truths in this book. It excites my heart to show you how God can work in your life as well if you are yet unconverted.

THE GREATEST DISCOVERY

Recently one self-deceived man came to me and said he had to talk. The urgency in his voice spoke volumes. The moment he walked into my study, he solemnly said, "Can I be a Christian and my life never change?"

This man was a "faithful" church member, a Sunday school leader, and a deacon who despite his apparent conversion to Christ ten years earlier had never experienced a change in his life. Although he had walked the aisle of our church, prayed the sinner's prayer, and been baptized, "nothing happened."

The problem was he had never come to Christ on His terms. He had never experienced a holy mourning over his sins. He had never humbled himself in God's presence, committing his life to Christ. He had never known any hunger for God's Word. He continued to live a life totally absorbed in himself. No wonder he had no peace.

By his own admission, he remained full of pride and arrogance, to say nothing of losing a twenty-year battle with pornography. The only consistent thing about his "Christian life" was the haunting doubt about his salvation. His question was a legitimate one: "Can I be a Christian and my life never change?"

"Of course not," I told him. "Whenever Jesus Christ invades a person's life, He comes in to take over and will reroute that life into a new direction at all costs."

SPIRITUAL RICOCHET

Grabbing a golf ball that was lying on the carpet, I threw it as hard as I could at the baseboard across the room. *Bam!* It ricocheted back at us with a loud sound like a gun exploding.

"That's a picture of a true conversion to Jesus Christ," I said. "When you come to faith in Christ, your life is like this golf ball hitting that wall. You were once proceeding rapidly in one direction only to run into the living Christ. When you come face to face with Jesus Christ, you cannot continue in the same direction. Your life will be rechanneled in a totally different direction. You cannot meet the Lord and continue in the way you were before."

After sharing Scripture with him for the next hour, I sensed that the soil of his heart was being plowed by the Holy Spirit. The seed of the Word was falling upon broken, fertile soil watered by his own tears.

With a broken voice, he said, "I am certain I'm lost and need to be saved. I have never humbled myself and submitted my life to Christ to be my Lord and Savior."

After years of fighting, he finally came to the end of himself, the only place where Christ can begin. As we bowed our heads together in prayer, this lost church member, this unsaved deacon, prayed to God, confessing his sin, committing his soul to Jesus Christ.

THE GREAT CHANGE

I must tell you, the peace of God instantly flooded his heart as he collapsed back exhausted in his chair. The heavy yoke of sin had been removed. Jesus Christ had now entered his life to inaugurate His sovereign rule. This man's conversion was, in reality, a coronation.

As he peered at the distant wall where my golf ball had rebounded back to us, he understood that this was precisely what had occurred in his life. After years of pursuing sin, he was now headed in a new direction. After traveling the broad path, he had now been rerouted onto the narrow path that leads to life.

And he was absolutely sure.

This is but one of many devout, church-attending people I have seen come to know Christ as Savior and Lord. And in each case, there is assurance because their life is radically changed. When Jesus Christ moves into one's heart, He gives a brand-new life—not an upgraded version of one's old life. "If any man is in Christ, he is a new creature; the old things passed away; behold, new things have come" (2 Corinthians 5:17). It is this transformation that breeds assurance.

As we proceed to our study of 1 John, may God give each of you who know Christ a deep confidence that you possess eternal life. Make no mistake about it—if you are saved, God wants you to know that you are. And you can!

But for others of you, the message of this book needs to strip away the thin veneer of your false assurance and reveal that you have never been born again. If this describes your life, may the truths in 1 John lead you to repent of your sins and put your complete trust in Christ alone to save you.

May you find no peace until you find your peace in Him.

Chapter three

INTIMACY WITH THE ALMIGHTY

Vital Sign #1: Communion with Christ

1 JOHN 1:1–4

*Do we know Him?...It does not mean a general, superficial
acquaintance; there is an intimacy about it, a knowledge in a
special sense; it is a personal acquaintance, an intimacy.*

Martyn Lloyd-Jones

*L*ong before they were America's Team, the Dallas Cowboys were my team.

When the famed NFL franchise began play in the fall of 1961, I was a ten-year-old fourth-grader living in nearby Fort Worth. I lived in a world of imagined gridiron glory, playing on a peewee football team that was the Texas state champion.

As you can imagine, Sunday afternoon trips to watch the Cowboys play in the Cotton Bowl were bigger than life, especially as they played the likes of the Cleveland Browns with Jim Brown and the New York Giants with Y. A. Tittle.

But the biggest thrill of all was watching the hometown Cowboys. Mostly discards from other NFL rosters, they nevertheless loomed huge in my young eyes. And coaching these upstart Cowboys was the one I put on the highest pedestal—Tom Landry. Always calm and neatly dressed on the sidelines, Coach Landry epitomized the aura of the Cowboys. In fact, he was the Cowboys.

As the years progressed, my love for Coach Landry and the Cowboys only grew. So you can imagine my excitement, some seventeen years later, when I had the opportunity to meet "the only coach the Cowboys had ever had."

I'll never forget going to the high-rise building where the Cowboys had their offices and introducing myself to the receptionist, who had me wait a few minutes, causing my anticipation to mount higher.

Then came my moment. I was now going to meet the man I had known about for so long. Coach Tom Landry walked out and ushered me into his office, which was decorated with all the accomplishments of the Cowboys' dynasty. As I sat down across the desk from him, face to face with the man I had read so much about, I was struck with what a privilege this was. Having read all about him and having admired him from afar, now meeting and knowing Coach Landry was a cherished moment.

KNOWING OR KNOWING ABOUT?

Coming to know Jesus Christ is much like what I have just described. For many of you, you have grown up admiring Him, reading about His greatness, and knowing about Him. But there must come a time when you finally meet Him and come to know Him. There must come a personal encounter where you enter into a relationship with Him. It is one thing to know *about* Him but something else entirely to actually *know* Him. Do you know Jesus Christ? Or do you merely know about Him? There is a huge difference!

The one who genuinely knows Christ has a personal, intimate relationship; the one who only knows about Christ simply possesses a few historical facts. Unfortunately, many people know about Jesus in the same way they know about other historical figures. Their supposed faith in Christ is like their knowledge of, say, George Washington. They may know all about George Washington without ever having met him. They have read books or heard lectures about our first president. They know he was the father of our country, where he was born, where he lived, what he did and said, how he affected history, and when he died. There's no doubt that they believe the leader of the American Revolution really existed. They admire him, respect him, even revere him. They celebrate an annual holiday that honors his birthday. But they don't know him, not personally.

Many people know all about Jesus Christ as a historical figure. They know He was a carpenter from Nazareth, that He was born in Bethlehem, that He came as the Son of God to become the Son of Man, that He died upon a cross for our sins. With much certainty, they believe that He really existed—no doubt about it. They admire Him, respect Him, and even celebrate a holiday once a year that honors His birthday. They know all about Him—they just don't know Him personally.

To know Christ means more than acknowledging historical facts about Him. It means having an intimate relationship with Him because He lives inside you. It means more than sitting in church, reading the Bible, singing hymns. Rather, it means the risen Christ lives within your heart and gives you eternal life.

ANOTHER JESUS

Such a personal relationship with Christ was lacking in the lives of many in the first century. A heresy called gnosticism had made inroads into the early church. The people who promoted this heresy presumed they possessed special knowledge from Christ about the kingdom of God. But this knowledge was at best folly and at worst deadly.

The gnostics taught that all matter was evil and only what is spiritual and ethereal is good. They could not accept that Jesus came to earth in a physical body. A true incarnation, they claimed, would be evil. Thus, they denied Jesus' humanity and said He was actually a phantom.

As the apostle John starts his letter of 1 John, he must first carefully define who the real Jesus is. No apparition or ghost, the true Christ was fully man, someone with flesh and blood who could be heard, seen, and touched. John begins by affirming that the first mark of assurance for a true believer is experiencing a personal relationship—fellowship, John calls it—with Jesus Christ.

THE ETERNAL CHRIST

With breathtaking grandeur, the apostle writes:

> What was from the beginning, what we have heard, what
> we have seen with our eyes, what we beheld and our hands
> handled, concerning the Word of life. (1 John 1:1)

Using an expression similar to the one with which he began his
Gospel account of Jesus' life ("In the beginning was the Word," John
1:1), John writes that in the beginning of all things, He was already in
existence. Like the eternal God (1 John 2:13–14), Jesus existed from
all eternity past, long before His appearance here on the earth.

As the Creator of all things, Jesus Christ is the uncreated One who
preexisted before everything that has been created. "He was in the
beginning with God. All things came into being by Him, and apart
from Him nothing came into being that has come into being" (John
1:2–3). As the "eternal Father" (Isaiah 9:6), meaning Father of eterni-
ties, Jesus dwelt with the Father from all eternity past—without beginning, uncreated, eternal. The prophet recorded, "His goings forth are
from long ago, from the days of eternity" (Micah 5:2).

THE WORD BECAME FLESH

Two thousand years ago, this eternal One took upon Himself the
nature of a man and was born of a virgin (Luke 1:35). Deity stepped
out of eternity into time to become the God-man. Mystery of all mys-
teries, Deity condescended to become humanity. God became a man
in human flesh, fully God, yet fully man, as much God as though He
were not man, and as much man as though He were not God. Beyond
our ability to fully comprehend, "the Word became flesh, and dwelt
among us, and we saw His glory, glory as of the only begotten from
the Father, full of grace and truth" (John 1:14).

Writing to refute the gnostic heresy of his day, John says we heard
Him, saw Him, beheld Him, handled Him—He was a real man! Con-

tained in these verbs is the gospel in a nutshell. With their ears, John, along with the other disciples, heard Jesus speak words of eternal life. With his eyes, John saw Him live without sin, die upon the cross, and be raised from the dead. With his mind, he beheld Him, carefully studying and scrutinizing His life, claims, and death. With his hands, he actually touched Him. Not a phantom or ghost as the gnostics claimed, Jesus was a man. But more than a mere man, He was God in human flesh.

No secondhand religious experience, John and the apostles personally lived with Christ for over three concentrated years. But it was not simply their physical proximity to Jesus that transformed their lives. Their spiritual relationship with Him is what made the difference. More than merely know about Him, they knew Him! They committed themselves to Jesus Christ by faith as their Lord and Savior, and He became intensely real to them!

John had a personal relationship with Christ because he was born again. It is this very same encounter with Christ that John wants us to enjoy. By trusting Christ, we too can know Him and experience eternal life!

MADE KNOWN TO US

Although we have never seen Christ as John did, He is made known to us through John's witness to us. The apostle writes:

> And the life was manifested, and we have seen and testify and proclaim to you the eternal life, which was with the Father and was manifested to us. (1 John 1:2)

"The life," referring to the supernatural person of Christ, was not hidden but clearly revealed for all to see. Throughout his letter, John makes this life known to us as he gives a reliable, accurate account of what he personally heard, saw, and touched. When John says "testify" he means to give an eyewitness account of what he has observed. Here is the apostle's vivid testimony of the truth about the person and work of Christ which he experienced firsthand. As the "Word of life," Jesus came to reveal life—real life, eternal life, divine life. As the "eternal life," Jesus came to offer the very life of God. He is the life (John 14:6), the giver of life, the creator of life, and the sustainer of life—life which is eternal.

Jesus said, "I came that they might have life, and might have it abundantly" (John 10:10). Without Christ, we have a hollow, empty existence, but not life. Eternal life is knowing Christ in a personal way; it is a vital, living relationship with God through His Son that lasts forever (John 17:3).

PARTNERSHIP WITH CHRIST

At this point, John invites us to experience this life.

> What we have seen and heard we proclaim to you also, so that you too may have fellowship with us; and indeed our fellowship is with the Father, and with His Son Jesus Christ. (1 John 1:3)

Salvation is entering into fellowship with the Father and Jesus Christ. "Fellowship" (koinonia) means partnership. More than a mere social contact with another person, it is the formation of a joint venture together between two or more people. Originally, it pictured several men entering into a business together and working side by side, such as when John participated with Andrew, James, and Peter in a fishing business (Luke 5:7). They were "in the same boat together," casting the same nets, pulling in the same fish, sharing the same profits, weathering the same storms. That is what it means to enter into fellowship with Jesus Christ. It is entering into a partnership with Him in which we share our lives with Him and He with us. Having entered into intimate association with God through Christ, life is now lived as a joint venture with the Father, the Son, and the one who is genuinely converted.

This is remarkable! As wretched sinners, we have nothing in common with a holy God—absolutely nothing. We are unable even to come into His presence because of the defilement of our sins, and yet the blood of Christ cleanses us of all our sins (1 John 1:7, 9) and provides us access to Him. Because of the Cross, we may enter into partnership with God and daily live in closest fellowship with Christ.

By taking on humanity, Jesus was able to take upon Himself our sins at the cross (1 Peter 2:24). He came to earth that we might go to heaven. He was born of a virgin that we might be born again. He became the Son of Man that we might become sons of God. Through faith in Christ, we become "partakers of the divine nature" (2 Peter 1:4), and receive His imputed righteousness (2 Corinthians 5:21), life (John 14:21), peace (John 14:27), love (John 15:10), and joy (John 15:11). What a partnership!

COMING TO CHRIST

We enter by faith into this joint partnership of salvation. Eternal life is neither something we deserve nor earn by our good works. This relationship with Christ is a gift from God to all who will trust in His Son. Only by faith can we know Jesus Christ with a depth of relationship that is just as real as the fellowship John experienced with Christ two thousand years ago. Through believing in Christ, we too may spiritually hear, see, and feel Him today. This is why Peter says, "Though you have not seen Him, you love Him, and though you do not see Him now, but believe in Him, you greatly rejoice with joy inexpressible and full of glory" (1 Peter 1:8).

Through the pages of Scripture the words of Christ continue to speak to our heart with a voice far louder than any audible voice. Jesus said, "My sheep hear My voice" (John 10:27). The Spirit calls through the Word of Truth, amplifying the voice of Christ, and we respond by faith to follow Him just as John did two thousand years ago.

Likewise, we may see Him with the eyes of faith. Jesus said, "Blessed are the pure in heart, for they shall see God" (Matthew 5:8).

Although we do not see Him with our physical eyes, when we come to Christ with a humble, broken, meek heart that hungers for His righteousness (Matthew 5: 3–6), we see with the eyes of faith and Christ becomes far more real than if He were standing immediately before us.

And we may touch Him with the hands of faith. Whenever we read His Word or hear Him proclaimed to us, our hearts reach out and lay hold of Him by faith. We embrace Him with the arms of faith and feel His presence that seems just as real as if He were physically with us.

This is how intimate our personal fellowship is with Him. We walk with Him, talk with Him, and sense His presence with us. He lives within our hearts, never to leave us. As our ever-present companion, He comforts, counsels, guides, strengthens, and corrects us.

FELLOWSHIP WITH THE FATHER

When we enter into this relationship with Christ, we also enter into fellowship with God the Father. John writes, "Our fellowship is with the Father, and with His Son Jesus Christ" (1 John 1:3). We can't know one without knowing the other. Because God and Christ are one (John 10:30), a partnership with the Son involves a relationship with the Father as well.

What a glorious consortium! The fullness of the Godhead is our experience. We enjoy close communion with the Father and intimate fellowship with the Son. Describing the closeness of this relationship, Jesus said, "In that day you shall know that I am in My Father, and you in Me, and I in you" (John 14:20). It is difficult to fully grasp how close this partnership is. If the Son is in us, we are in the Son; and since the Son is in the Father, we are also in the Father. In other words, Christ indwells me, I indwell Him, and we both indwell the Father.

At the same time, John says, "You also may have fellowship with us" (1 John 1:3), meaning we also may enter into a special relationship with all others who know Christ. As believers in the Lord, we become one with everyone who is in Christ. A depth of fellowship exists between all who are followers of Christ. Our relationship in Christ transcends our differences as we are supernaturally fused together by the Spirit into the body of Christ. Not only are we connected to the Father and Son, but we are also one with all other believers.

THE GREATEST JOY!

There is no greater joy than knowing Christ and seeing others come to know Him and enter this wonderful fellowship. Thus, John concludes:

> And these things we write, so that our joy may be made complete. (1 John 1:4)

With exuberance in his heart, John writes this book so that his own joy may abound as others come to know Christ. The greatest pleasure in all the world is to enjoy fellowship with Christ. The second greatest is seeing others come to know Him. That's what John is saying here.

You and I will never know any true and lasting joy until we know Jesus Christ. He is the source of all joy, the only true fulfillment of our hearts. Through partnership with Him, He fills our lives with the fullness of His presence, and His joy floods our hearts. Jesus said, "These things I have spoken to you so that My joy may be in you, and that your joy may be made full" (John 15:11). The psalmist wrote, "In Your presence is fullness of joy; in Your right hand there are pleasures forever" (Psalm 16:11).

Why do we experience joy when we believe upon Christ and walk daily with Him? Everything else that follows in 1 John explains why. Although joy is specifically mentioned only here, those things that promote joy are described throughout the rest of the letter. Several avenues of joy open up to us when we have a relationship with Christ.

AVENUES OF JOY

Joy in knowing Christ (1:1–4). To know Christ is to enter into joy. Joy is not something we can fabricate; it is the by-product of Christ reigning in our hearts. Whenever Her Royal Highness Queen Elizabeth is in residence at Buckingham Palace, the royal flag flies over the estate. In the same manner, joy is the flag that flies over the castle of our heart when Christ the King is reigning.

Joy in confessing sin (1:5–2:2). In one way or another, all unhappiness is the result of sin. Only when we regularly confess our sin and daily walk in personal holiness do we know joy. A clean heart is a joyful heart. And when we sin, confession always replenishes our joy (Psalm 51:12).

Joy in obeying God (2:3–6). Obedience to God's Word always ushers us down paths of righteousness which lead to a deep heart satisfaction. Jesus said, "If you know these things, you are blessed if you do them" (John 13:17).

Joy in loving others (2:7–11; 3:14–18; 4:7–21). As God increases our love for others, our hearts are flooded with joy. A self-centered existence always steals our inner peace and contentment, but a selfless love multiplies joy within us. The more we sacrifice for others, the more satisfied we are. Love always leads to joy; wherever you find one, you will find the other.

Joy in refusing the world (2:12–17). The enticements of the world promise much joy but never produce. When we choose not to love the world but to love God, joy becomes ours in fullest measure. The pleasures of the world are temporary, but God's pleasures last forever.

Joy in knowing the truth (2:18–27; 4:1–6). God's truth leads to true joy because only the truth can set us free (John 8:32). False doctrine is a dead-end journey that always leads to despair and, ultimately, hell. The truth delivers and delights, but the devil's lies destroy and damn.

Joy in anticipating Christ's return (2:28–3:3). No event so excites our hearts as the longing for the return of Christ. Our lives are elevated above the futility of the daily grind as we lift up our heads because our redemption draws near.

Joy in practicing righteousness (3:4–10). The pursuit of personal holiness yields the fruit of joy. Our greatest pleasure is found in being conformed into the image of Christ who is our joy. Joy is the by-product of becoming like Him.

Joy in enduring persecution (3:11–13). Though the world of unbelievers opposes us for our faith, such affliction only increases our joy. Jesus said we are "blessed" (happy) when men persecute us for righteousness (Matthew 5:10–12) because such attacks purify us and drive us closer to Christ.

Joy in answered prayers (3:19–24). As we pray, we fellowship with God which increases our experience of joy. Living in close communion with God through prayer, as well as relying upon Him to care for us, removes burdens and increases blessings. As we see answers to our prayers, our joy is made complete.

THE JOYFUL ADVENTURE

As you can see, the entire Christian life is a joyful adventure of living in close partnership with Jesus Christ, sharing all that we are with all that He is, relying upon His resources, enjoying His presence. What joy is ours in Him!

This joy can be yours only when you are absolutely sure about your salvation. There can be no joy as long as you are unsettled about your eternal destiny. The most frustrated person in all the world is the person who wants to go to heaven but is not sure whether he or she will make it. Only when you are confident about eternity can you have joy today.

Do you know Christ intimately? Do you experience fellowship with God and His Son? Do you sense His presence in your life? Do you experience the exhilarating joy of a personal relationship with Him? True believers do.

ARE YOU IN THE GAME?

Many months after preaching this passage and all its rich truths to our church family, a businessman in our church set up an appointment to see me.

As he began to share his reason for coming, he said there was missing from his life "whatever it is that everyone else has." Everyone else, including his wife, seemed to "be in the game," but he was empty on the inside.

As he was searching for the words to express himself, I suspected it was the reality of Jesus Christ that was missing from his life. He had experienced church, but not Christ. He had religion, but not a relationship with Him.

"It's as though you've been sitting in the stadium Sunday after Sunday," I explained, "watching from the corner of the end zone, but you've never gotten into the game down on the field."

"So how do I get into the game?" he asked.

"That's easy. That's what the Cross is all about," I told him. "Jesus came to this earth to die for our sins. It's as if one end of His cross is planted on the fifty-yard line, and the other end reaches all the way up into the corner of the end zone where you are sitting. What you must do is take a step of faith and come to Christ. If you will confess your sins and commit your life to Him, He will receive you, lead you down onto the field, and put you into the game. You will become a part of God's team."

"What if I fail Him and fumble the ball?" he asked.

"Don't worry, Jesus will live in you and through you. When you're tackled, He'll pick you up. If you drop the ball, He'll pick it up and put it back in your hands. Ultimately, you can't lose. You're going to win because He's already won the victory for us."

If he had been sitting any farther forward on my couch, he would have fallen onto the carpet as I spoke.

"Would you like to get into the game?" I asked.

"Absolutely," he said. "That's what I want more than anything else."

We bowed our heads and he prayed, surrendering to Jesus Christ, confessing his sin, committing his life—and receiving the free gift of eternal life.

In that moment, this man went from the grandstands to a place in God's starting lineup. Jesus was now real in his life, and a whole new ball game had begun. Christ's victory had become his victory.

WHAT ABOUT YOU?

This could happen in your life. You need to know Christ. Do you have a settled conviction that you are a true child of God? Is the assurance of salvation your precious possession? More than an assurance about God's existence, do you know that Christ lives within your heart? Moments after you die, will you be with the Lord in glory?

If you want to be on God's team, then commit your life to Him. The Cross reaches out to where you are right now.

Get in the game.

Chapter four

DEALING WITH THE SIN WITHIN

Vital Sign #2: Confession of Sin

1 JOHN 1:5–2:2

No one can see what sin is till he has learned what God is.

J. I. Packer

A flippant youth once asked a preacher, "You say that unsaved people carry a weight of sin. I feel nothing. How heavy is sin? Is it ten pounds? Eighty pounds? A hundred pounds?"

"Let me ask you something," the preacher inquired. "If you laid a four-hundred-pound weight upon a corpse, would it feel the load?"

"It wouldn't feel anything because it's dead."

"So it is with the soul that is spiritually dead," the preacher said. "It, too, feels no heavy load of sin. Such a person is indifferent to its burden of sin and uncaring about its presence."

The youth was silenced.

A DEEP AWARENESS OF SIN

When true conversion occurs, the sinner, unlike this young man, feels the heavy weight of sin pressing upon his convicted heart. Seeing himself as spiritually bankrupt before a holy God, he no longer covers his sins but openly confesses them. The heart convinced of sin now eagerly confesses it to God, trusting in Christ's sacrifice alone for forgiveness.

Whenever God performs a true work of saving grace, it is always accompanied by a deep awareness of one's sin. Without the conscious awareness of one's sin, there is no perceived need for forgiveness from sin. Only when a person feels the heavy burden of sin, leading to the confession of that sin, does salvation occur. And only as one continues to confess his sin over and over can he experience the assurance of his salvation.

So confession of sin is the second vital sign necessary for the assurance of our salvation. First, as we saw in the last chapter, the awareness of an intimate personal relationship with Jesus Christ leads to the assurance of one's salvation. Now, second, the awareness of sin in one's life leading to the confession of that sin to God breeds assurance. People who are spiritually dead feel no conviction of sin. Therefore, a deep sense of one's own sin becomes a major component in possessing a certainty about one's salvation.

HOLY, HOLY, HOLY

The apostle begins by declaring the absolute holiness of God. Until we see the sinless perfection of God, there will be no awareness of our own sin.

> This is the message we have heard from Him and announce
> to you, that God is Light, and in Him there is no darkness
> at all. (1 John 1:5)

This imagery of light portrays God's holiness in a way that is unmistakable. Just as light is pure, undefiled, and without any darkness, so God Himself is absolutely pure, morally perfect, and without any imperfections. Consequently, God's holy character becomes the universal standard by which He judges each one of us. God demands, "You shall be holy, for I am holy" (Leviticus 11:44; 19:2; 20:7; 1 Peter 1:16). And Jesus said, "You are to be perfect, as your heavenly Father is perfect" (Matthew 5:48).

When measured by the divine perfection of God's holiness, we all fall infinitely short of God's glory. The Bible says, "All have sinned and fall short of the glory of God" (Romans 3:23). Not one of us is morally perfect as God is. Because God is holy, an irreconcilable chasm exists between Him and sinful men that cannot be bridged by our good works or self-made religion. The closer we view ourselves in light of God's holiness, the more we see our unholiness.

WOE IS ME!

Such was the experience of the prophet Isaiah. When King Uzziah died, Isaiah was enabled to see God in a vision, enthroned in the heavens, majestic and transcendent over all. The prophet then heard the seraphim crying out to one another, "Holy, holy, holy" (Isaiah 6:3).

The foundations of the temple began to shake, but not nearly as much as Isaiah's heart. Smoke engulfed the temple, symbolizing God's holiness, wrath, and judgment.

The prophet cried out, "Woe is me, for I am ruined! Because I am a man of unclean lips...for my eyes have seen the King, the LORD of hosts" (6:5). Seeing God's glory revealed Isaiah's own unworthiness, which deserved judgment. Because of this awareness of the Lord's holiness, the prophet was stricken with shame over his sin. Such is the trauma of holiness.

I AM A SINFUL MAN!

Peter had a similar experience on the Sea of Galilee. After fishing all night and catching nothing, Jesus told this disciple to go back out and cast his nets again.

Reluctantly, Peter followed Christ's instruction. When he did, a great number of fish were caught, so many that the nets broke and his boat began to sink. Other boats summoned to help pull in the catch began to sink, too.

When Simon Peter saw that display of Christ's glory, "he fell down at Jesus' feet, saying, 'Depart from me, for I am a sinful man, O Lord!'" (Luke 5:8).

Like Isaiah, Peter came to the deep realization of his own sin when confronted with the holiness of the Lord. This revelation of Christ's deity made him painfully aware of his sinfulness and of his unworthiness to be in the Lord's presence.

It will be the same with you and me. Whenever we come face to face with Jesus Christ and His glory, we too will be brought to a deep awareness of our sin. To enter into the presence of God is to stand in the blazing light of His holiness. No one can stand in such divine light without becoming painfully aware of his or her sin. Jesus noted, "And this is the judgment, that the light is come into the world, and men loved the darkness rather than the light; for their deeds were evil. For everyone who does evil hates the light, and does not come to the light, lest his deeds should be exposed" (John 3:19–20).

COUNTERFEIT CHRISTIANS, BEWARE!

If someone claims to be a Christian but does not deal with his sin, John says, that person is not saved. He has no fellowship with God whatsoever.

> If we say that we have fellowship with Him and yet walk in
> the darkness, we lie and do not practice the truth. (1 John 1:6)

Those who *say* they have fellowship with God claim to be Christians. They verbally confess Christ, professing to know Him. But if their lives remain in darkness—if they live in disobedience and unconfessed sin—they are lost. Regardless of how sincere they may be, such a claim to be a Christian is a sham. Because this person is in the darkness, he cannot see the sin in his own life nor realize his lost condition. The darkness blinds him to the reality of his unconverted condition.

If you don't walk in the light of God's holiness, it is a sure sign that you have never believed in Jesus Christ. If one's walk does not match his or her talk, such a confession is a lie. No matter how much a person may claim to know Christ, if he remains in the darkness, he is separated from God, oblivious to his lost condition.

WALKING IN THE LIGHT

By contrast, the one who is truly converted to Christ gives evidence of this reality by walking in the light. This person has entered into true fellowship with Christ as a result of the profound awareness of his own sin. It is the knowledge of sin which drives him to Christ for cleansing. John writes:

> But if we walk in the Light as He Himself is in the Light, we have fellowship with one another, and the blood of Jesus His Son cleanses us from all sin. (1 John 1:7)

Walking in the light represents a habitual lifestyle of living in personal holiness. The metaphor of walking implies an ongoing process over an extended period of time. It suggests movement, direction, and one's behavior. Walking in the light pictures one living in God's truth and holiness on a regular, consistent basis. Lest there be any misunderstanding, this speaks *not of the perfection of one's life, but the direction of it.*

As one walks in the light, the deeds of darkness are exposed, leading to the confession of sin. It is only in God's light that one can see his own sin and properly deal with it, seeking forgiveness. The one who walks in the truth of God's holiness readily confesses his sin and receives daily cleansing from Christ's blood.

THE GREAT COVER-UP

Unfortunately, many who claim to be Christians have never forsaken their sin. They continue in their sinful lifestyle as if nothing is wrong. It is of these pretenders that John writes:

> If we say that we have no sin, we are deceiving ourselves, and the truth is not in us. (1 John 1:8)

Amazingly, this self-deceived person claims to have no sin problem, remaining blind to the depravity of his own life. Although God says, "All have sinned and fall short of the glory of God" (Romans 3:23), this person denies it. Sin—what sin? He just doesn't see it. It's not that he thinks he is too bad to be saved, but too good. Unfortunately, his morality may keep him out of jail, but it will not keep him out of hell.

How can someone be so self-deceived? It is because he has never seen himself in the light of God's perfect holiness which alone can reveal his sin. As long as he remains ignorant of God's holiness, he cannot see the truth about himself.

This self-righteous one is always comparing himself with others and concluding he is acceptable to God. Of course, he measures himself by someone who is outwardly immoral and concludes he himself must be right with God. This counterfeit Christian is wrapped in a cloak of self-deception. Believing he is saved, he is tragically lost.

NO PLACE FOR TRUTH

Regarding such a person, "The truth is not in [him]," John concludes. He may have gone through the empty motions of a so-called religious conversion, but he has never been born again. The truth about his own sin is not to be found in him. That's because the truth about God's holiness is sadly missing. No one can be saved until they know they are lost. Jesus died for sinners, not self-righteous people. Until a person sees his own wretched sin, he can never be saved. Not until he sees the depravity of his own soul will he flee to Christ for cleansing and forgiveness.

A great preacher was teaching on the subject of depravity. At the end of his sermon, a listener approached him and said, "I can't swallow what you say about depravity."

"That's all right," the preacher responded. "It's already inside of you."

Such is the problem of all humanity. The defilement of sin is already within us. Like the venom of a deadly snake, the poison of sin is pulsating through our mortal flesh and must be treated. If we fail to deal with the sin within us, we shall perish and be eternally lost.

CONFESSING SIN

Contrary to the counterfeit Christian, the one who is genuinely converted regularly confesses his sin. He is convicted of his sin and agrees with God about it, which is what confession is all about. John continues:

> If we confess our sins, He is faithful and righteous to forgive us our sins and to cleanse us from all unrighteousness. (1 John 1:9)

The one who walks in the light is aware of his sin and must have relief from his guilt by confessing it to God. In the light, his sin is clearly exposed. He senses his need for forgiveness and delights in confessing it to God in order to receive His cleansing.

Confessing sin is common to all believers. Confession means to agree with God about our sin. It is acknowledging our sin to God, admitting that we have violated His holiness, and asking for His forgiveness. Confession is the act by which we assume responsibility for our sin and deal with it God's prescribed way. Until sin is confessed, there can be no true fellowship with a holy God.

WHATEVER HAPPENED TO SIN?

Our world has a skewed view of sin. Someone has written:

> Man calls it an accident;
> God calls it an abomination.
> Man calls it a blunder;
> God calls it a disease.
> Man calls it a chance;

God calls it a choice.
Man calls it an error;
God calls it an enmity.
Man calls it a fascination;
God calls it a fatality.
Man calls it an infirmity;
God calls it an iniquity.
Man calls it a luxury;
God calls it leprosy.
Man calls it a liberty;
God calls it lawlessness.
Man calls it a trifle;
God calls it tragedy.
Man calls it a mistake;
God calls it madness.
Man calls it a weakness;
God calls it willfulness.

NECESSARY FOR SALVATION

Entrance into God's kingdom is marked by confession of sin. Jesus established this when He began the Sermon on the Mount by saying, "Blessed are the poor in spirit, for theirs is the kingdom of heaven. Blessed are those who mourn, for they shall be comforted" (Matthew 5:3–4). Declaring one's spiritual bankruptcy and weeping over personal sin is necessary for entrance into His kingdom.

In the parable of the Pharisee and the tax-gatherer, the self-righteous Pharisee never saw his own sin and remained outside God's kingdom (Luke 18:9–14). But the tax-gatherer was so overwhelmed by his own sin, he sensed his own unworthiness to come before a holy God and was unwilling to even lift up his eyes to heaven because of his separation from God. He beat his breast, condemning himself, and said, "God, be merciful to me, the sinner." He saw himself not merely as *a* sinner, but *the* sinner. No one could be further away from God, he assumed, than he. Such a humbling confession of sin marks everyone who is justified before God.

After conversion, the confession of sin continues throughout one's Christian's life. Consider the apostle Paul. As he grew spiritually, so did awareness of his own sin. First, he saw himself as "the least of the apostles" (1 Corinthians 15:9), then "the very least of all saints" (Ephesians 3:8), and finally, the "foremost of all" sinners (1 Timothy 1:15). As Paul matured in the Lord, he grew in the awareness of his sin. This is the mark of one who is truly saved.

The difference between the true and false convert is not whether or not they sin. They both will sin. But when the genuine believer lapses into sin, he loathes it; the counterfeit Christian leaps into sin and loves it. The real Christian confesses sin; the false one covers it up (Proverbs 28:13).

MAKING GOD A LIAR

The one who fails to confess his sin, no matter how much that person may claim to be a Christian, is not a genuine believer. The apostle writes:

> If we say that we have not sinned, we make Him a liar and His word is not in us. (1 John 1:10)

One may claim to be a Christian, but if there is no awareness of personal sin, that person is not saved. With perfect insight, he may see sin in the lives of others, or may protest against the ills of society, but if he is blind to the wretched sins of his soul, he is lost. Until there is confession of his own sin, there is no forgiveness for his sin.

What is worse, when he says, "I have not sinned," he makes God a liar! Without equivocation, God says he has sinned.

The person who denies his sin reminds me of the college freshman who went to the dorm laundry room with his dirty clothes all bundled up in an old sweatshirt.

He was so embarrassed by how dirty his clothes were that he never opened the bundle. Instead, he pushed the bundle into a washing machine and when the machine stopped, he pushed the same wadded-up bundle into a dryer. Finally, he took the still unopened bundle back to his room, where he discovered that his clothes had gotten wet, then dry, but not clean.

Even so, many go through the external, empty motions of religion, concerned with what others think, careful not to reveal their sin, but they never bring their sin out into the open before God. They never confess their sin and, therefore, never come clean before God.

If such a self-deceived person mourns over his sin, it is only because of what it has done to hurt himself, not because of how it has grieved God. For example, Judas was sorry for his sin, but hanged himself in remorse and went straight to hell. Such a person never sees that it was his sins that nailed Christ to the cross. Always playing the "blame game," he is quick to point out sin in others but never acknowledges his own sins to God, much less be broken over them.

AN ADVOCATE WITH GOD

Returning to the true believer who confesses his sins, John explains the great provision for sins in the atonement of Jesus Christ. Even though believers will continue to sin, God has provided the means by which His holy anger toward our sins may be appeased.

> My little children, I am writing these things to you so that you may not sin. And if anyone sins, we have an Advocate with the Father, Jesus Christ the righteous; and He Himself is the propitiation for our sins; and not for ours only, but also for those of the whole world. (1 John 2:1–2)

Speaking in legal terms, John says that when charges are brought against us, we have a lawyer to represent us before God. Seated at the right hand of God, Jesus intervenes as our defense attorney, defending us against all charges brought by Satan. Although the devil accuses us before God day and night for our sins (Revelation 12:10), Jesus is our Advocate, pleading His blood before the Father. The Son's perfect sacrifice at the cross has propitiated, meaning satisfied or appeased, the righteous anger of God against our sins.

As Christians, we will continue to sin even after our conversion, but Jesus Christ remains our Advocate. He died for our sins and is the pacifier of God's wrath toward our sins. Even though we are guilty, we confess our sin and are cleared of all charges and immediately forgiven. A genuine believer will habitually practice a lifestyle of confessing his sins and receive God's full acquittal through the blood of Christ.

WHERE DO YOU STAND?

How are your vital signs? Have you passed or failed this important test? The person who is truly saved is the one who, having seen the light of God's holiness, senses the wickedness of his own soul and confesses his sin to God, seeking His forgiveness based upon the perfect sacrifice of Christ for our sins. Does this describe you?

A counterfeit Christian has no regard for his sin. He experiences no conviction of sin, no remorse that leads to repentance, no confession of sin. His life is one big cover-up of his sin. But a true believer is convicted of his sin and confesses it to God, first at his conversion and then on a regular basis throughout his Christian life.

- Do you realize that you are a sinner who falls short of God's holiness?
- Do you understand that your sin has separated you from God?
- Do you see your need for God's forgiveness and cleansing?
- Have you confessed your sin to God?

- Are you willing to forsake all your sin?
- Do you walk in the light of personal holiness as a continuing life pattern?
- Do you understand that Christ is the only provision for your sin?
- Have you truly believed upon Him alone to receive the forgiveness of your sin?

If you can answer yes to these questions, then you can enjoy the assurance of your salvation. But if there is a nagging doubt over whether or not you belong to Him, maybe there is a reason for that haunting feeling. Maybe you still need to deal with your sin before God.

If you will truly believe upon Christ, confessing your sins, and cast yourself upon His mercy, you can be saved and enter into the joyful assurance of your salvation. Why don't you turn from your sins right now and turn to Him who is willing to forgive you?

If you will, He will.

WHAT THEN?

William Gladstone was one of Great Britain's foremost leaders during the nineteenth century. Not only was he a brilliant statesman, he was also a devout Christian. One day, a young man came to Gladstone to talk about his future. As the two sat across the desk from each other, Gladstone asked the young man what he proposed to do.

He replied he was interested in going to Cambridge or Oxford University to pursue a good education.

Gladstone said, "That's good. A man needs a good foundation and I think that is wise. What then?"

"Well, sir, I thought that when I graduate from college I could get a job in one of the law firms and gain some practical experience because there are things that I'll learn there that I'll never learn in school."

"That's wise, that's very wise. What then?"

"What I'd really like to do is serve in government, and if I do well in law, perhaps one day I can stand first seat in Commons and be involved in the governing of the world through the government of Great Britain."

Gladstone said, "I appreciate that. We need men in government who are here because they are dedicated to a cause. That's splendid. What then?"

"Well, sir, I thought if I did well with my party that perhaps sometime along the way they might choose me to be prime minister—to sit where you sit and to make an impact that way."

"Well, somebody has to sit here. That's good that you're going to aim that high. What then?"

"Well, sir, I have been keeping a diary and I suspect that if I'm able to do these things, I could write my memoirs and pass on to other folks like myself the lessons that I've learned along the way."

"That's good. That can be a real help to folks. I think that's wise. What then?"

"Well, sir...like any man, I guess it would be time for me to die."

"Yes, whether all your goals are achieved, no matter where you sit, ultimately we are reduced there. What then?"

"Well...I have been so busy making my plans that I haven't had much time for religion. I do plan to get around to it, but I hadn't really thought about that. That's, you know, just not been in my thinking."

William Gladstone stood up and said, "Young man, you'd better get right home. Get down by the side of your bed, open up your Bible, and think life through to its very end."

WHAT NOW?

After you have lived your life and come to the end, what then? Jesus said, "What does it profit a man to gain the whole world, and forfeit his soul? For what shall a man give in exchange for his soul?" (Mark 8:36–37). The ultimate "buy high, sell low" proposition is to live your life for the things of this world and then come to the end of your days only to discover that you will lose it all.

If you have Christ, you have everything. But if you die without Christ, you have nothing.

Chapter five

THE EXPEDIENCE
OF OBEDIENCE

Vital Sign #3:Commitment to God's Word
1 JOHN 2:3–6

Faith that saves has one distinguishing quality: saving faith is a faith that produces obedience; it is a faith that brings about a way of life.

Billy Graham

What our Lord said about cross-bearing and obedience is not in fine type. It is in bold print on the face of the contract.

Vance Havner

*D*uring the Civil War, no man in the South was more deeply revered nor highly respected than General Robert E. Lee. History records that on one occasion Lee sent word to his most loyal and devoted officer, General Stonewall Jackson. The message simply said that the next time Jackson rode in the direction of Lee's headquarters, the commander of the Confederate army would be glad to see him regarding a matter of minor importance.

Upon receiving the message, Jackson immediately made preparations to depart early the next morning. Rising before sunrise, he saddled his horse and rode the eight miles to Lee's headquarters through a driving snowstorm.

Jackson arrived just as Lee was finishing breakfast. Surprised to see him so soon, Lee inquired, "Why have you come at such an hour through such a terrible storm?"

"You said you wished to see me," Jackson said. "General Lee's slightest wish is my supreme command."

Stonewall Jackson grasped the monumental importance of obedience to one's superior, no matter how insignificant it may appear. This is the same with any command of Christ for us. It is a truth that every believer in Jesus Christ must clearly understand.

OBEDIENCE IS NONNEGOTIABLE

In the Christian life, as in the military, obedience is not incidental, it's fundamental. Obedience is not a peripheral issue, but a primary issue. The necessity of obedience lies at the very heart of what it is to be a good soldier of Jesus Christ. As our Commander, our exalted Lord's every desire must be our supreme command.

At the heart of what it means to be a Christian is living a life of obedience to God. Having begun the Christian journey with an initial step of obedience to the gospel, every subsequent step on the narrow path is marked by obedience to His commandments. It is this continued obedience that is so necessary for the assurance of our salvation.

By no means do I mean to imply that we become sinlessly perfect. Nor do I mean that we never disobey God again. John himself wrote, "If we say that we have no sin, we are deceiving ourselves and the truth is not in us" (1 John 1:8). Sad to say, isolated acts of disobedience will still occur in the life of every believer, and for some, there may even be extended seasons of carnal behavior. But conversion to Christ does produce a new lifestyle of obedience that can be clearly seen. We can know we are genuinely saved as we see ourselves walking the path of obedience to God.

Assurance of salvation becomes real not by looking to a past event, such as walking an aisle, but by observing our present obedience to the Word of God.

OBEDIENCE BRINGS ASSURANCE

In the last two chapters, we considered the first two vital signs of a converted life: a personal relationship with God through Jesus Christ

(1 John 1:1–4) and sensitivity to personal sin leading to the regular confession of sin (1 John 1:5–2:2). Now, the apostle brings us to the third sign of our assurance—obedience.

> By this we know that we have come to know Him, if we keep His commandments. The one who says, "I have come to know Him," and does not keep His commandments, is a liar, and the truth is not in him; but whoever keeps His word, in him the love of God has truly been perfected. By this we know that we are in Him: the one who says he abides in Him ought himself to walk in the same manner as He walked. (1 John 2:3–6)

There are two kinds of people who claim to know Christ—first, those who truly know Him (2:3, 5–6) and, second, those who claim to have a relationship with Him but do not (2:4). Those in the first group, John says, give clear evidence of God's saving grace in their lives through their obedience to His commandments. Those in the second group say they know Christ but fail to obey Him, invalidating their confession. Like a counterfeit twenty-dollar bill, they may appear genuine but they are not.

ABSOLUTE ASSURANCE

Assurance of your salvation must have no leaks. Like an automobile tire bleeding air, holes in your assurance will impede your progress in the Christian life and leave you flat. The only real assurance is "airtight" because a life of obedience, as we shall see, is inseparably bound to experiencing true assurance of salvation.

> By this we know that we have come to know Him, if we keep His commandments. (1 John 2:3)

Only by keeping Christ's commandments can we be absolutely sure that we actually know Him. Clearly, God wants us to know Him.

But further, He also wants us to know that we know Him. The first comes by faith, the latter by an ongoing lifestyle of obedience. As we carefully examine verse 3, we observe four components of obedience that are always connected to true saving faith.

OBEDIENCE BEGINS AT CONVERSION

First, *saving faith involves immediate obedience.* As soon as we come to faith in Jesus Christ, we begin to live in obedience to Him. John does not say, "By this we know that we have come to know Him, if we begin living obediently within a decade, or within a year, or within a month." Emphatically, John says, "We know that we have come to know Him, if we keep His commandments." This implies that from the very moment one is converted to Christ, he will begin to live a life of obedience to God. No delay or time lapse will exist between the time of our conversion to Christ and when we begin to obey Him. When faith begins, obedience begins.

Unfortunately, all too often I hear a personal testimony that goes something like this, "I received Jesus as my Savior when I was ten years old, but I didn't begin to obey him as my Lord until I was twenty." Such a testimony violates what the Scripture is teaching in this verse. One begins to know Christ when he begins to obey Him.

THE GOSPEL IS TO BE OBEYED

The gospel itself is a command to be obeyed, not a suggestion to be considered. The Bible says, "Jesus came into Galilee, preaching the gospel of God, and saying...'Repent and believe in the gospel'" (Mark 1:14–15). Jesus' gospel invitation was an imperative command calling for immediate obedience—believe! Elsewhere, John writes, "He who believes in the Son has eternal life, but he who does not obey the Son shall not see life, but the wrath of God abides on him" (John 3:36). In this verse, *believe* and *obey* are used interchangeably. To believe in Christ is to obey Him. Not to believe in Him is to disobey Him.

Those who first believed in Christ obeyed the gospel. Of the early converts of the first church, we read, "The word of God kept on spreading; and the number of the disciples continued to increase greatly in Jerusalem, and a great many of the priests were becoming obedient to the faith" (Acts 6:7). Previously lost, these Jewish priests were being converted to Christ by becoming obedient to the faith. Keeping God's Word began when they obeyed the gospel.

What was true of these first conversions to Christ is true today. No one can become a Christian and be disobedient to the gospel that commands the sinner to "repent and believe." The rich young ruler who came to Christ wanted eternal life, but he was unwilling to obey Christ and remained unconverted (Matthew 19:21–22). He wanted the blessings and benefits of salvation but refused to submit his life to the demands and requirements of Christ's Word, thus departing as he came—lost. Neither can we believe in Jesus Christ without submitting our lives to His Word.

OBEDIENCE IN ALL AREAS

Second, *saving faith involves comprehensive obedience.* When John says, "By this we know that we have come to know Him, if we keep His commandments," his use of the plural *commandments* is of monumental significance, emphasizing all of them, not just an isolated few.

When one is saved, it is not a selective obedience into which he enters. Rather, our new heart has a desire to be completely obedient to all the commandments of God. Partial obedience is no obedience. At conversion, the entirety of one's life comes under the entirety of God's Word. The true believer doesn't go through God's Word cafeteria style, picking and choosing what commands he wants to keep and passing over the others. Rather, the one who is truly saved responds like Joshua to God's command: "This book of the law shall not depart from your mouth, but you shall meditate on it day and night, so that you may be careful to do according to all that is written in it" (Joshua 1:8). The true Christian commits all that he is to all that Christ is, and this includes all that He commands. No true Christian will select which commandments he wants to obey and refuse the others. If he refuses His commandments, Christ will refuse him.

But we may "know that we have come to know Him" if we are committed to obeying *all* His commandments. If salvation begins when we choose to obey Him, assurance begins when we observe this obedience in our lives.

OBEDIENCE THAT IS DILIGENT

Third, *saving faith involves diligent obedience*. In this same verse, John says we must "keep His commandments." In the original language, *keep* conveys the idea of a guard or watchman watching over a very priceless treasure. In like manner, the true believer will be diligent to carefully guard all that God's Word requires in order to do it. To him, God's commandments are not burdensome (1 John 5:3), but a blessing (Psalm 1:1–3). He obeys them, not because he has to, but because he wants to—the evidence of a new heart.

In Psalm 119, a remarkable psalm that speaks of the primary place God's Word occupies in the life of the believer, we read how diligently we should keep His commandments. David writes, "Thy word I have treasured in my heart, that I may not sin against Thee" (verse 11). "I shall delight in Thy statutes; I shall not forget Thy word" (verse 16). "I shall run the way of Thy commandments, for Thou wilt enlarge my heart" (verse 32). "Give me understanding, that I may observe Thy law, and keep it with all my heart" (verse 34). Diligent obedience occurs as we treasure and delight in the commandments, running to keep them with all our heart. This is not the mark of the super-Christian, but every Christian.

OBEDIENCE UNTO THE END

Fourth, *saving faith involves steadfast obedience*. When John writes, "we keep His commandments," *keep* is in the present tense, meaning a continual obedience to God's Word that will carry to the end. All true believers will experience an enduring obedience to God that will be sustained over time. Despite the hostile opposition of the world, the flesh, and the devil, God will continue to work in the true believer and guarantee a firm obedience, faithful to the end.

Could someone start the Christian life with an immediate obedience but fall away before the end of his life and turn his back on God? Not according to this verse. The one who is truly born again will persevere in obedience throughout his life. On the other hand, the one who starts well but later abandons his commitment to obey gives evidence that he was never truly saved. As it has been well said, "The faith that fizzles before the finish had a flaw from the first." Real faith will continue on into the future all the way to the finish (Hebrews 3:14, 18).

ALLEGIANCE TO A NEW MASTER

The apostle Paul writes that obedience always accompanies saving faith. When one is saved, there is a transfer of allegiance from the old master, sin, to a new Master, Jesus Christ. Paul reasons, "Do you not know that when you present yourselves to someone as slaves for obedience, you are slaves of the one whom you obey, either of sin resulting in death, or of obedience resulting in righteousness?" (Romans 6:16). Paul states a general axiom that is obvious to all: slaves are bound to total obedience to their masters.

By way of application, Paul states, "But thanks be to God that though you were slaves of sin, you became obedient from the heart to that form of teaching to which you were committed, and having been freed from sin, you became slaves of righteousness" (6:17–18). Everyone, Paul argues, is either a slave of sin or a slave of righteousness. Before we came to know Christ, we were slaves of sin and lived in obedience to sin. But now we are converted to Christ and He is our new Master. As slaves of Christ, we now live in obedience to Him with a God-given passion to obey His Word.

EMPTY WORDS, EMPTY LIVES

As we return to 1 John, we are warned about those who claim to know Christ yet do not obey Him. In no uncertain language, John denies such people actually know Christ.

> The one who says, "I have come to know Him," and does not keep His commandments, is a liar, and the truth is not in him. (1 John 2:4)

This could not be any clearer. The faith that *says* but does not *obey* is really unbelief in disguise. When John says this person fails to "keep His commandments," he means there is no immediate, comprehensive, diligent, steadfast obedience. The person who confesses Christ without living in obedience to Him is living a self-led life with himself at the center of his own universe, running his own life, following his own agenda, and doing whatever he wants, whenever he wants, wherever he wants with little or no regard for God's Word. Such a deceived person does not know Christ.

Moving a step further, John writes that the one who says he knows Christ but does not obey His commandments is a liar. That's strong language! His confession of Christ is fraudulent and fictitious. Since he is a liar, he is the son of the father of all lies, the devil himself (John 8:44) and certainly not God's child. Although he claims to know Christ, every time he opens his mouth to tell someone about his supposed relationship with Christ, he speaks a lie. Every testimony he gives is a lie, every hymn or chorus he sings is a lie, every prayer he prays is a lie. He gives the appearance of believing in Christ when, in reality, he does not. He awakens every morning to live the lie!

No wonder John says of such a person, "The truth is not in you."

ALL TALK, NO WALK

Consider Judas who heard the truth like no other, having the Scriptures taught to him by the greatest Teacher who ever lived, the One who was the embodiment of truth itself—Jesus Christ. Day after day, Judas journeyed with Christ from one village to the next as our Lord discussed the eternal truths of the kingdom of God along the way. No one had closer proximity to the truth than he did.

Deeply involved in all aspects of ministry, Judas was even commissioned by Jesus to preach the truth. As one thoroughly immersed in Scripture, he heard the truth, studied the truth, learned the truth, and proclaimed the truth. He trafficked in truth every day for over three years. But there was one problem.

He was lost.

This well-taught disciple knew all the truths of the kingdom of God, but he never submitted his life to the authority of it. He saw others obey the truth, yet he himself never did. He witnessed other lives transformed by it, yet he himself remained unchanged. To this day, he remains the ultimate example of one who gives every outward appearance of being saved but in reality is lost.

FAITH WITHOUT WORKS?

Addressing this same issue head on, James writes, "What use is it, my brethren, if a man says he has faith, but he has no works? Can that faith save him?" (James 2:14). Can someone who says he is a Christian have true saving faith and yet live in constant disobedience to God? Is it possible to have faith and yet not obey God? Can faith that is without obedience save? The answer is so obvious that James does not even bother to answer it. Clearly, faith without works is dead!

James gives an illustration: "If a brother or sister is without clothing and in need of daily food, and one of you says to them, 'Go in peace, be warmed and be filled,' and yet you do not give them what is necessary for their body, what use is that?" (2:15–16). Here is another rhetorical question, the answer of which is so obvious, James need not even answer it. Words without works are worthless!

Faith that talks the talk without walking the walk, he writes, is merely hot air. It is faith in name only. In other words, faith alone saves, but faith that is alone does not save. True saving faith is always accompanied by the works of obedience. If one has faith deeply rooted in Christ, the budding fruit of obedience will grow and blossom and be clearly seen.

James understands that some will want to think they are saved without having to validate it by their good works. Anticipating this objection, he writes, "But someone may well say, 'You have faith and I have works; show me your faith without the works, and I will show you my faith by my works'" (2:18).

DEVIL FAITH

With wit surpassed only by his God-given insight, James responds to such an absurd position, saying, "You believe that God is one. You do well; the demons also believe, and shudder" (2:19). If someone says, "I believe, I believe," but never lives in obedience to it, James says, "You're no different than the devil. Even he knows and believes the truth, but doesn't obey it." This pseudofaith is merely intellectual assent without making a personal commitment. It is only acknowledging the truth, not submitting to it.

Consider how James attempts to sober such a person. "But are you willing to recognize, you foolish fellow, that faith without works is useless?" (2:20). Do you not see that faith that stands alone without obedient works is empty, dead, nonsaving faith? The faith that does not lead to obedience is the faith that does not lead to heaven.

Christendom is filled with people who have Bibles full of notes, calendars full of church activities, and heads full of knowledge, but empty lives void of salvation as evidenced by no obedience to Christ. Such people are merely going through the empty motions of religion, devoid of a saving relationship with Him. The one who is saved, James says, is not merely a hearer of the Word, but a doer of it (James 1:22–26)

OBEDIENCE PRODUCES MATURITY

Returning to 1 John, we discover that, on the other hand, the one who places himself under the authority of God's Word and obeys it experiences two realities: spiritual maturity and assurance of salvation.

> But whoever keeps His word, in him the love of God has truly been perfected. By this we know that we are in Him. (1 John 2:5)

John reminds us that the one who obeys God's Word is advancing in spiritual maturity. When he writes that God's love is "perfected in us," he means we experience His love more fully and deeply as we obey Him. The word *perfected* carries the idea of fruit being brought to ripeness. To the extent that a believer obeys God, he will experience God's love in richer measure. The one who is genuinely saved will be seeing an ongoing spiritual growth in his life marked by greater levels of obedience.

When John says, "By this we know that we are in Him," he is saying we can know we are rightly related to Christ as we grow in our comprehension of God's love. The resulting spiritual growth, in turn, provides a deeper assurance of our salvation.

THE MASTER OF OBEDIENCE

As John brings this discussion of obedience to a close, he points us to the ultimate example of obedience—the Lord Jesus Christ Himself. If we claim to be followers of Christ, then we will live in obedience because that is how He lived.

> The one who says he abides in Him ought himself to walk in the same manner as He walked. (1 John 2:6)

If I read this verse correctly, all who claim to know Christ will follow Him and live as He lived—not perfectly but purposefully. In fact, the word *Christian* means one who resembles Christ. The life of a genuine Christian will resemble Christ's life, which at its core includes a life of obedience.

As the Son of Man, Jesus' earthly life and ministry were marked by obedience; He always lived in perfect obedience to the will of the Father. Jesus said, "I can do nothing on My own initiative. As I hear, I judge; and My judgment is just, because I do not seek My own will, but the will of Him who sent me" (John 5:30). On another occasion, Jesus said, "For I have come down from heaven, not to do My own will, but the will of Him who sent me" (John 6:38). This commitment to obedience continued to the very end. On the eve of His crucifixion, Jesus prayed, "Not My will, but Thine be done" (Luke 22:42). From start to finish, Christ lived a life of total obedience to God.

As a result, it only stands to reason that if you say you know Him, obedience will characterize your life. When Jesus said, "Follow Me," implicit in that command was the call to follow Him in a life of obedience to God's Word. Plain and simple, if you're following Him, you will be obeying Him.

STANDING AT THE CROSSROADS

Examine your own life. Do you love God's commandments? Is your desire to submit yourself to them? Do you gain great pleasure in obeying God? Are you grieved and convicted when you disobey Him? Is it the delight of your heart to obey God's Word? Do you confess your sin when you disobey God?

If you are genuinely born of God, you will answer affirmatively to these soul-searching questions, and you will have the assurance of your salvation. An obedient life is a truly converted life.

Perhaps you could not give a positive answer to these questions. Maybe you find yourself obedient to sin, not to God. Maybe you are resisting God's Word rather than gladly submitting to it. Maybe you cannot describe your heart as a heart of obedience.

If so, you need a new heart.

Chapter six

WHEN LOVE
GETS REAL

Vital Sign #4: Compassion for Believers

1 JOHN 2:7–11; 3:14–18; 4:7–21

He who does not love his brother has, in fact,
no brother to love for he is not a child of God at all.

Henry Alford

Under the reign of Oliver Cromwell in seventeenth-century England, a soldier was condemned to die, a public execution to be carried out that very night at the ringing of the curfew bell.

This soldier was betrothed to a beautiful young woman who appeared before Cromwell and pleaded with him to spare her lover's life. But all was in vain. Her fiancé would die that evening.

The preparations were finalized for the execution, and the city awaited the sounding of the bell at curfew. When the time came, the sexton, who was old and deaf, put both hands upon the rope and pulled it with all his might. But the bell did not ring. He continued pulling again and again, unaware that no sound was coming from the bell.

Unknown to all, this soldier's fiancée had climbed to the top of the belfry and wrapped herself around the tongue of the huge bell. As the sexton pulled the rope, she was smashed against the sides of the bell, her body absorbing the blows and muffling the sound. When the bell ceased to swing, she came down from the tower wounded and bleeding before the watching eyes of the amazed crowd.

Cromwell, who waited a short distance from the place of execution, was perplexed. Had his orders been defied? He demanded an explanation of why the bell had not tolled.

As Cromwell questioned his officers, this young woman was dragged before him. She cast herself at Cromwell's feet and confessed what she had done. With tears streaming down her cheeks, the young girl showed her bruised and bloodied hands.

The display of her love overwhelmed Cromwell. "Go your way," he said. "Your lover lives. Curfew will not ring tonight."

DO YOU KNOW LOVE?

True love pays any price for the one loved. It stands ready to sacrifice all, even at great personal risk, in order to seek the best for another. This is how Christ loved us. Jesus died in our place, bearing our sins in His body and absorbing the wrath of God, that we might be spared eternal death. He extends His nail-pierced hands to us, unworthy sinners that we are, and offers to receive us from our sentence of eternal death.

In response to such perfect love, this is precisely how we are to love others. We can know Christ truly lives within us when we see His love permeate our hearts. If love fills our hearts, then we can be absolutely sure that we have been converted to Christ. One of the primary evidences that we have been genuinely converted to Jesus Christ is our display of sacrificial, selfless love for fellow believers. Assurance of salvation becomes real when love gets real.

FROM HATRED TO LOVE

Take, for example, Saul of Tarsus. No one opposed and threatened the early church more than this fiercely religious man who was lost. Filled with an unholy fury, he hated true believers with a vengeance. But God knocked Saul off his high horse—literally. Christ appeared to him and he was born again.

After his conversion to Christ, do you think Saul could have continued to arrest and kill the Christians? No way! The new birth so revolutionized his life that he was gripped with a new love for the very Christians he had previously sought to destroy. The love of God burst through his once-hardened heart as he reached out to all people with the gospel of Jesus Christ. At Lystra, Paul preached and the people stoned him, dragged him outside the city, and left him for dead (Acts 14:19). But Paul was so full of love that he got up and went back into the town to finish the sermon. He was willing to pay any price— even risking death—that they might believe.

ALL BELIEVERS ARE LOVERS

Like pictures developed from the same negative, what was true of Paul's life will be true of all who are genuinely born again. Through the miracle of regeneration, our stubborn heart of unbelief is invaded by sovereign grace and drawn into fellowship with Christ. In that moment, "The love of God has been poured out within our hearts through the Holy Spirit who was given to us" (Romans 5:5).

Like a mighty overflowing river, God's love fills and floods our hearts because of our faith in Jesus Christ. Because we have received God's love, we now have a new capacity and desire to love others. We cannot help but love others—Christ is alive within us!

LOVE IS A CHOICE

It is that love for others that the apostle John discusses as he outlines our responsibility to love fellow believers.

> Beloved, I am not writing a new commandment to you, but an old commandment which you have had from the beginning; the old commandment is the word which you have heard. On the other hand, I am writing a new commandment to you, which is true in Him and in you, because the darkness is passing away and the true Light is already shining. (1 John 2:7–8)

This commandment is God's mandate to love others. Love is a commandment from God, a choice of the will, an act of obedience. It is not an option; it is an obligation binding upon every believer. More than a feeling, love is an act of obedience that results in our sacrifice for others. Although the world's idea of love centers on sentimental emotions and warm feelings, we are commanded by God to love others whether we feel like it or not.

There are times when our feelings toward someone else just aren't there. Some people are easier to love, others are more challenging. Some Christians are like porcupines—they've got a few good points, but they're hard to get close to! But our love toward such people must be unconditional and transcend personality differences, social backgrounds, or even petty, personal offenses. In fact, the greatest act of love is to reach out to someone who is hard to love or who can do nothing for us in return. Our love becomes real when we choose to move beyond our comfort zone and love the unlovely, even to the point of making a personal sacrifice for their highest good.

A NEW STANDARD OF LOVE

John, called the apostle of love, now writes, "On the other hand, I am writing a new commandment to you" (2:8). Jesus raised the old standard of love to a higher level. Instead of loving others as we love ourselves, now we are to love them as Christ has loved us. Jesus said, "A new commandment I give to you, that you love one another, even as I have loved you" (John 13:34). It should be obvious that Christ loves us more than we love ourselves. In the ultimate act of love, He laid down His life for us—unconditionally, sacrificially, perfectly, and completely. Jesus then said, "This is My commandment, that you love one another, just as I have loved you. Greater love has no one than this, that one lay down his life for his friends" (John 15:12–13). We are to love one another sacrificially—as Christ has loved us.

When John says this new commandment "is true in Him and in you" (1 John 2:8), he means if Jesus is real in your life, so will His love be real in you. Wherever Christ lives, there also His love abides. It cannot help but shine through us.

Like a sailboat tacking in the breeze, the entire orientation of our life has been redirected away from self and toward God and others. God poured out His supernatural love into our newly converted heart, supplying us with an enormous reservoir of love. Where we once focused upon ourselves, we now reach out to others in love. Not perfectly, mind you, but practically, we do love other people.

John adds, we must love "because the darkness is passing away, and the true light is already shining" (verse 8). This world is a dark place, devoid of real love, but when Jesus Christ, the light of the world, came (John 8:12), His love came shining into the darkness. As Christ indwells us, the light of His love shines through us, extinguishing the darkness of this world.

HOW'S YOUR LOVE LIFE?

Let's get personal. Who's hardest for you to love? Who has hurt you the most lately? Who really irritates you? Who is most difficult for you to forgive? I hope you have a picture of him or her in your mind, because the greatest act of love will be for you to reach out to that person in patience, kindness, and forgiveness.

Christ's love was uniquely demonstrated when He went to the Cross. I doubt He felt warm fuzzies toward the people who were spitting on Him, whipping Him, and crushing a crown of thorns onto His head. But He chose to say, "Father, forgive them, for they know not what they do." Christ's love was a choice of the will, and so it must be for us. Love is a commandment to be obeyed, not a feeling to be followed.

CONFESSION WITHOUT COMPASSION

Unfortunately, many people who claim to be Christians show little love for others. They continue to live in their small, self-centered world and rarely venture outside of it for the benefit of others. Though religious and involved, they remain unconverted and their lack of love verifies this. They *say* they love God, but the fact that they do not love others betrays their confession of Christ. In very blunt language, John says:

> The one who says he is in the Light and yet hates his brother is in the darkness until now.... The one who hates his brother is in the darkness and walks in the darkness, and does not know where he is going because the darkness has blinded his eyes. (1 John 2:9, 11)

To say you are in the light is to claim to be a Christian. If you are genuinely born again, you are going to love other Christians. It follows as day follows night. If you claim to be a Christian but have no love in your heart for others in the church, then John says you're in the dark in spite of your claim to be in the light.

No excuses, please! If my life is not marked by unconditional love, I am living in the darkness, no matter how much I may claim to be in the light. Regardless of how many times I have been baptized, read the Bible, or prayed, if there is no love for a brother or sister in Christ, I am still living in the darkness and am in dire need of the light of the new birth.

Of this lost, professing Christian, John says pointedly, the "darkness has blinded his eyes." This person who claims to know the Lord but has no love for others is blind to the lost condition of his soul, blind to his need for the gospel, blind to his selfishness, blind to his lack of love, blind to his lostness, and blind to the fact that he will face God in the final judgment.

Martyn Lloyd-Jones, the great expositor for many years at Westminster Chapel in London, writes on this verse,

> Because he is an unloving person, he causes other people to stumble. These people with this unloving nature are always finding problems and troubles. They always see insults where they do not exist. There is always something upsetting them.

They are always being put out. They are constantly stumbling because of their unloving spirit. But, says John, they cause other people to stumble also, because they are in this state and condition. No one knows what to do with them. They are always touchy and sensitive, and they constantly run other people into trouble.

Our churches are filled with such people. They claim to know Christ, are actively involved in the church and engaged in its ministries, but they remain in darkness and fail to recognize that the light of Christ's love does not shine through them. They are carnal, self-willed, short-tempered, demanding, impatient, and, truth be known, lost.

WHEN LOVE IS REAL

In contrast to the counterfeit Christian, there is one who genuinely loves Christ and, therefore, genuinely loves other people. This person's love knows no limits; it knows no boundaries. Such a person reaches out to love all people, even those who are hard to love.

The one who loves his brother abides in the Light and there is no cause for stumbling in him. (1 John 2:10)

It is unnecessary for this person to say he belongs to Christ. It is obvious that he is saved by the way he loves. The testimony of his life comes through loud and clear. He doesn't go through life keeping score with people; he forgives. He doesn't exist to be served; he serves.

People who are heaven-bound are so overwhelmed with what God has done for them that it becomes natural—really, supernatural—to do loving deeds for others. They do not go through life inflicting harm on others or causing them to trip and fall. These people have such love that their tongue, attitudes, actions, and reactions are under the control of God.

The one who is genuinely saved graciously works to get along with others. He is patient, kind, not jealous, not boastful, not arrogant, not rude, not self-seeking, not easily angered, forgiving, gracious, and finds no pleasure in someone else's sin (1 Corinthians 13:4–6). Such a person is easy to identify. No wonder Jesus said, "By this all men will know that you are My disciples, if you have love for one another" (John 13:35).

LOVE MAKES IT OBVIOUS

Lest we forget the significance of love, John reintroduces this theme in chapter 3. Love is a repeated emphasis in this letter because it is an accurate means of diagnosing where we are spiritually.

> By this the children of God and the children of the devil are obvious: anyone who does not practice righteousness is not of God, nor the one who does not love his brother.... We know that we have passed out of death into life, because we love the brethren. He who does not love abides in death. Everyone who hates his brother is a murderer; and you know that no murderer has eternal life abiding in him. (1 John 3:10, 14–15)

This is crystal clear! If anyone says he or she believes in Christ but does not love others, this person is a child of the devil; he is lost and unsaved. One's spiritual state, John says, is clearly revealed by the presence or lack of love. The one who does not practice love "abides in death"—that is, does not possess eternal life. Where there is no supernatural love, we can only assume there is no spiritual life.

LOVING LIKE JESUS LOVED

John continues on the theme of love by defining what true love looks like:

> We know love by this, that He laid down His life for us; and we ought to lay down our lives for the brethren. Little chil-

dren, let us not love with word or with tongue, but in deed and truth. (1 John 3:16, 18)

Pointing us to the cross, John says, "This is what love is—real love." It was there that Jesus laid down His life for the sheep. He didn't simply tell us, "I love you." Rather, He voluntarily laid down His life as an offering for our sins. What a demonstration of love as He sacrificed everything for us, wretched sinners that we were!

In those last hours before His death, He suffered a mockery of justice, was slapped in the face, and had a crown of thorns pressed onto His head. He was beaten with a rod, He absorbed the blows of men's fists, His back was ripped open with a whip, and then He carried His cross through the streets of Jerusalem—all because He loved us. In the crucifixion itself, He persevered through it all—the intense pain, bruised flesh, loss of blood, muscle cramps, dehydration, hunger, and heat exhaustion—all because He loved us. He became the sin bearer crushed under the heavy load of our guilt, all while He absorbed the fierce wrath of God poured out upon Him for our sins—all because He loved us.

With Golgotha as the backdrop, John calls us to love one another in like manner. Our love must never be merely "with word or with tongue," but "in deed and truth," as demonstrated by Christ (3:18). We must lay down our lives for others, giving of ourselves to seek their highest good. In so doing, we are to relinquish personal comforts, withstand personal attacks, forgive all offenses, withhold any retaliation, and seek only the best for others regardless of how they treat us (Romans 12:17–21). This is Christ—this is love!

All who have received the Lord will live like this. Not perfectly, not completely, but this kind of love will be seen shining through their lives. Paul admonishes us, "Walk in love, just as Christ also loved you, and gave Himself up for us" (Ephesians 5:2). This is not mere religious talk, but how God expects every believer to live. Indeed, every true believer will live like this in varying degrees—no exceptions.

LOVE IS FROM GOD

Such selfless, supernatural love can never well up from within us. It must be given to us from above. Like a priceless family heirloom being passed down from a father to his son, so is this love from our heavenly Father imparted to us.

> Beloved, let us love one another, for love is from God; and everyone who loves is born of God and knows God. (1 John 4:7)

When we were regenerated by the Holy Spirit, God put his divine nature within us (2 Peter 1:4). Because the nature of God is love, it also becomes our nature to love as well. Loving fellow Christians comes naturally to the believer because he has a new nature from God which is marked by love.

Additionally, we are indwelt by the Holy Spirit at our conversion. At that time, the love of God is poured out within our hearts by the Holy Spirit (Romans 5:5), who begins to produce the fruit of love in our lives (Galatians 5:22). As a result, the one who is born of God loves other Christians because love is from God.

NO LOVE? NO GOD!

John makes the point again, no matter how much a person may say he is a Christian, he is not genuinely saved if love is not present:

> The one who does not love does not know God, for God is love.... If someone says, "I love God," and hates his brother, he is a liar; for the one who does not love his brother whom he has seen, cannot love God whom he has not seen. (1 John 4:8, 20)

If there is no love in my heart for other people, I cannot possess love for God. Love for God and love for others are two sides of the same coin. Wherever one is found, so is the other. Love for others flows out of love for God. But if love for others is missing, then love for God is nonexistent.

Pause for a moment and take a hard look at your life. Behind your claim to be a Christian, do you possess genuine love for other people? Do you really? Are you a kind and forgiving person? Do you consider the interests of others more important than your own? Do you see yourself reaching out to people who are hard to love?

Self-examination is critical. The clear, concrete evidence of love in my life provides the truest confirmation that I genuinely belong to God. No matter how much I say I believe in Christ, only when I see love in my life for God, as well as for others, can I have the confidence that I have truly been born again.

IF GOD SO LOVED US

A God-like love is a love like God showed us when He gave His Son to die for our sins.

> By this the love of God was manifested in us, that God has sent His only begotten Son into the world so that we might live through Him. This is love, not that we loved God, but that He loved us and sent His Son to be the propitiation for our sins. Beloved, if God so loved us, we also ought to love one another. (1 John 4:9–11)

It is clear from these verses that we are to love others as God has loved us, but how did the Father love us? In the greatest act of love, God gave up His only begotten Son to save hell-bound, hostile rebels such as you and me. We often think of the sacrificial love of Christ at the cross, and rightfully so, but here it is the sacrificial love of God the Father that ought to grip us. It was the Father who sent His Son to be crucified by the very people He loved. "God so loved the world, that He gave His only begotten Son" (John 3:16). Let that sink in afresh.

How great must have been the Father's love to part with His Son and watch Him be brutally put to death by those He was sent to save.

He gave His Son to be the atoning sacrifice for our sins when His wrath burned with holy anger against us. It was while we deserved hell that God offered up His Son. He took the initiative and loved us in spite of ourselves. If God had waited to love us in response to our love for Him, He would never have loved us. He simply chose to love us as a free exercise of His sovereign will, praise His name.

This is how we are to love others. Without waiting for others to reach out to us, we are to initiate love toward them, even to those who are offensive to us. When others harm us or injure our feelings, we must choose to love them. Even when our righteous anger is rightfully aroused, we must not let it keep us from reaching out to others.

LOVE PRODUCES ASSURANCE

John concludes that we can be absolutely sure that we are in God and He in us as we observe His love manifested in our lives.

> No one has beheld God at any time; if we love one another, God abides in us, and His love is perfected in us. By this we know that we abide in Him and He in us, because He has given us of His Spirit. (1 John 4:12–13)

Although God cannot be seen, we nevertheless can see Him revealed through our lives when we love others. I can see that God is real in my life and abides in me when His love grows and matures within me, reaching out to others. It is by the expression of divine love "perfected [brought to maturity] in us" that we know that we reside in God and He resides in us. His love is never stagnant in us, but ever transforming us and always prodding us to grow and deepen in that love.

> We have seen and testify that the Father has sent the Son to be the Savior of the world. Whoever confesses that Jesus is the

Son of God, God abides in him, and he in God. We have come
to know and have believed the love which God has for us.
God is love, and the one who abides in love abides in God,
and God abides in him. (1 John 4:14–16)

There are two ways to know that God lives in us and we in God.
One is by confessing Jesus Christ; the other is by abiding in God's love.
We can know that we have genuinely confessed Christ if we abide in
His love, and we know we abide in His love when His love is extended
through us to others. We can know that our confession of Christ is real
as we see God's love produced in us for others. The one who abides in
love is the one who abides in Christ.

By this, love is perfected with us, so that we may have confidence in the day of judgment; because as He is, so also are we
in this world. There is no fear in love; but perfect love casts
out fear, because fear involves punishment, and the one who
fears is not perfected in love. (1 John 4:17–18)

Reinforcing this same truth, John says the assurance of salvation
may be ours as we see love for others flow from our lives. We may
have confidence in our relationship with God, face the coming day of
judgment without fear, and know that our faith is real as we see that
our love for others is real.

A LOOK INWARD

These straightforward truths about love are a cause for self-examination
in all our lives. With soul-searching transparency, we must look carefully
for the evidences of God's supernatural love within us. Only as we discover such love within us can we have a true assurance of salvation.

Has the supernatural love of God flooded your soul and given you
a sacrificial love for others? Has God's love become real in your life?
Do you reach out to people and love them with a new patience and

forgiveness, or do you still harbor resentment and nurse grudges?

Does your love go beyond mere feelings to sacrificial service and sensitive concern, or do you continue to live in an utterly self-focused way? Do you have a real concern for others, or are you still callous and indifferent toward them?

A genuine believer is marked by genuine love. Only as our love for others is real can we be absolutely sure that our conversion to Christ is real.

Assurance is real when love gets real.

Chapter seven

NO TURNING

BACK

Vital Sign #5: Change of Affections
1 JOHN 2:12–17

He is no fool who gives what he cannot keep to gain what he cannot lose.

Jim Elliot

*I*t was the spring of 1519, and the famous explorer Hernando Cortés had secured eleven ships and seven hundred men from the governor of Spain. Armed with this sizable armada, he set sail from Europe to discover the New World.

His transatlantic voyage took several months, and upon his arrival in Veracruz, Cortés performed two dramatic acts that left an indelible impression upon his men. First, he planted the flag of Spain upon the sandy beach of the New World, claiming this land for his sovereign. Then he issued a command that shook his men to the depths of their souls. Before their watching eyes, Cortés ordered all eleven ships anchored in the bay to be burned.

The message was clear: there was no turning back. All ties to their past were severed. No possibility existed of returning home. Their only option was to press forward into the uncharted interior of Mexico and meet whatever might come their way.

BURN YOUR BRIDGES!

This is the commitment we must make to Jesus Christ. When we come to faith in Him, we plant the cross within our heart and stake a claim for our newly enthroned King. All escape routes leading back to the world are severed. All ties to our past way of life are burned. This step of faith breaks our old loyalties and establishes a new allegiance to Christ. The old has passed away; new things have come.

The greatest miracle that God performs is the miracle of the new birth. Regeneration radically alters the direction of our lives and changes the affections of our hearts. Before conversion, all people were hostile toward God and entrenched in the world. But salvation totally reverses the orientation of one's life. The one who once opposed God now loves Him. And the one who once sought the world now shuns it.

This change of one's desires is powerful proof of a true conversion to Christ. We can enjoy a greater level of the assurance of our salvation to the extent we see this change of desires within our heart. What we once loved, we now loathe. And what we once were indifferent toward, we now embrace. Now dead to the world, we are alive to God.

Truth abounds in the chorus, "I have decided to follow Jesus, no turning back, no turning back. The world behind me, the cross before me, no turning back, no turning back." This is the dramatic U-turn God works in our hearts through the glorious transformation of the new birth. The one who has truly believed in Christ has renounced the world and all its vain charms, has broken past allegiances, and has dissolved old loyalties in order to establish a new commitment to a new Master—Jesus Christ.

CONVERSION: THE GREAT CHANGE

Such was the case in a man named Zaccheus. As a chief tax collector, he was a supervisor over many other agents and was raking in money in excessive amounts, all at the expense of his own countrymen. Publicans were notorious for collecting more taxes than required. No doubt Zaccheus was participating in this abuse of absorbing the things of this world.

But one day he met Jesus Christ and his life was radically changed. Passing through Zaccheus' town, Jesus said He wanted to meet with him in his house. In the course of that brief encounter, Zaccheus was converted and his life revolutionized. He became a follower of Christ.

In response to this new commitment, Zaccheus said, "Behold, Lord, half of my possessions I will give to the poor, and if I have defrauded anyone of anything, I will give back four times as much" (Luke 19:8).

What a change! Having previously lived to accumulate the things of this world, Zaccheus now released his grip on them and returned them to the people. The glitter of the world had lost its allure in the heart of this newly converted man. Love for God now replaced love for the world.

Has such an about-face ever occurred in your heart? Do you have a growing love for God? Have you turned your back on the world in order to follow Christ? Many say they know Christ, but how many have severed their ties with their old world?

In our next look at the book of 1 John, the apostle records for us the fifth proof that brings the assurance of our salvation: a radical change of affections that God produces in the heart of the one who is born again. Old loves for the world decreases and new love for God increases.

SECURED AND ASSURED

As John begins this new section, he reminds us that our assurance is based upon the full and free forgiveness that is ours in Jesus Christ. It is through His death that we are secured and assured.

> I am writing to you, little children, because your sins have been forgiven you for His name's sake. (1 John 2:12)

There are only two families in the world—God's and Satan's. The new birth ushered us into God's family and rescued us from the devil's. Because our sins are forgiven, we are now a part of God's spiritual family. Never forget, forgiveness of our sins is the greatest gift of all to receive. What we could never achieve for ourselves, God provides freely for us through Christ's work at the Cross. All believers are the recipients of God's forgiveness, not because we deserve it, but solely for Christ's sake.

A NEW INTIMACY WITH GOD

Although all believers are forgiven, we are nevertheless at different stages of spiritual growth, a truth that John now recognizes.

> I am writing to you, fathers, because you know Him who has been from the beginning. I am writing to you, young men, because you have overcome the evil one. I have written to you, children, because you know the Father. (1 John 2:13)

John outlines for us the three basic levels of spiritual growth in Christ. All believers start at the *infancy level*. New believers have only the basic awareness of who God is, what He has done on their behalf, and what He is doing in the world. As a little baby first comes to know his or her parents, so a spiritual babe begins at this basic place of being introduced to God and growing to love Him and rest in His protection and care.

The second level of spiritual development could be called the *infantry level*. Believers at this level have matured to the place that they do battle with Satan, the evil one. They are in the battle for Christ as they oppose the devil.

The third level, what I call the *intimacy level,* is made up of those most advanced in spiritual growth. These know God at a deeper level than do spiritual babes. They have grown from their initial understanding of God to become spiritual fathers who "know Him who has been from the beginning." They have an intimate understanding of His eternality, sovereignty, and majesty.

So spiritual growth is a development from one level of fellowship with God to the next. Initially, we know Him as our Father, but we grow to know Him as the Sovereign of the universe. Through each phase, we grow to love Him more and more, thus fulfilling the greatest commandment: that we love God with all our being (Matthew 22:37).

A GREATER COMMITMENT TO GOD

As we grow spiritually closer to God, we also grow in our commitment to serve Him.

> I have written to you, fathers, because you know Him who has been from the beginning. I have written to you, young men, because you are strong, and the word of God abides in you, and you have overcome the evil one. (1 John 2:14)

John has already explained that spiritual fathers, or those most mature in the Lord, know God intimately as the eternal, uncreated, always existing One who rules over all. John now addresses the young men in the Lord, those at the second level of maturity, as those who are spiritually strong. More fully developed, their faith is stronger than in the infancy stage. Their convictions toward truth are deeper, their spiritual muscles are stronger. They are strong against sin and Satan. They are the "infantry" who do battle against the forces of darkness.

These young men are strong because the Word of God abides in them. It is God's Word, a sharp, two-edged sword, that fortifies their faith and makes them such a powerful force for God. As a result, they overcome the wiles of the devil and repel his advances. All this leads to a growing, deeper knowledge of God in the intimacy stage.

Make no mistake about it, only the new birth could bring about such a dramatic change. Those who were once aliens and enemies of God, working in cooperation with Satan, have now become children of God who do battle against the enemy they once served.

THE LOVE GOD HATES

John now issues a straightforward warning without any qualifications, exceptions, or escape routes:

> Do not love the world nor the things in the world. (1 John 2:15)

Just as clearly as God has commanded, "You shall not steal," "You shall not murder," and "You shall not commit adultery," He states, "Do not love the world nor the things in the world." This imperative allows no room for negotiation.

What exactly is "the world"? The Bible uses the term *world* (*kosmos*) in a variety of ways. First, it refers to the physical planet—the mountains, rivers, trees, beaches, and oceans. Second, *world* is used to refer to the mass of people who live on this planet. The Bible says, "God so loved the world, that He gave His only begotten Son, that whoever believes in Him shall not perish, but have eternal life" (John 3:16). Third, *world* refers to the false philosophies, ideologies, values, lifestyles, and religions that exist independent of and in opposition to God. It is this world John warns us not to love.

As "the ruler of this world" (John 12:31), Satan is orchestrating together all its various parts—the world of politics, the world of education, the world of entertainment and so on—into one massive rebellion against God. Under Satan's control, unsaved man creates his godless rules, establishes his humanistic values, and seeks his self-indulgent pleasures apart from God.

Martyn Lloyd-Jones defines the world when he writes,

> It must mean the organization and the mind and the outlook of mankind as it ignores God and does not recognize him as God and as it lives a life independent of God—a life that is based upon this world and this life only. It means the outlook that has

rebelled against God and turned its back upon God. It means, in other words, the typical kind of life that is being lived by the average person today who has no thought of God, no time for God, but thinks only of this world and this life and thinks in terms of time and is governed by certain instincts and desires. It is the whole outlook upon life that is exclusive of God.

Everything about this present world system is anti-God and functions apart from God. A man-centered, humanistic view runs this world and puts man in the center, relegating God to a lesser, subordinate role, or leaving Him out altogether.

HE'S GOT THE WHOLE WORLD IN HIS HANDS

This cosmic rebellion against God is masterminded by Satan, the prince of this world (John 12:31), the god of this age (2 Corinthians 4:4), and the ruler of the power of the air (Ephesians 2:2). He holds the entire world under his sway. The Bible says, "The whole world lies in the power of the evil one" (1 John 5:19). In other words, he's got the whole world in his hands. He is the author of all the world's lies, the conspirator behind all its murders and violence, and the power behind all its thrones as he holds all unbelievers within his grasp to do his will (2 Timothy 2:25–26).

To love the world is to seek the world's applause, adopt its values, crave its pleasures, and follow its philosophies. While we may appreciate the things of this world, use things, buy things, sell things, and look at things, we are not to love things. Instead we must love God. When we live for the things of this world, our heart is diverted from devotion toward God.

While those in the world are consumed with the acquisition of things, true Christians keep things in proper perspective. Our primary pursuit is the kingdom of God (Matthew 6:33). We may possess things, but things must never possess us.

COUNTERFEIT CHRISTIANS, BEWARE!

It is within this context of warning against worldliness that John issues an even stronger warning:

> If anyone loves the world, the love of the Father is not in him.
> (1 John 2:15)

If I read this verse correctly, love for the world and love for God cannot coexist in the same heart. These two loves are mutually exclusive and diametrically opposed to each other. Either love for God will drive out love for the world, or love for the world will displace love for God. The two cannot reside within the same heart. A world-loving Christian is a contradiction, an oxymoron. One may say he knows Christ, but if he continues to love the world, the love of the Father is not in him.

Conversion is a fork-in-the-road experience. The paths to two kingdoms lay before us—the kingdom of this world and the kingdom of God. To choose one is to refuse the other. No one can travel both roads at once.

ONLY ONE MASTER

Addressing the superficial religion of His day, Jesus made it abundantly clear that no one can live simultaneously for God and for this world: "No one can serve two masters; for either he will hate the one and love the other, or he will be devoted to one and despise the other. You cannot serve God and wealth" (Matthew 6:24).

Conversion is the exchange of one master for another. Having once lived under the mastery of money and in slavery to the things of this world, the one who chooses to enter the kingdom of God must follow a new Master, Jesus Christ. Love for God begins when love for the world is renounced.

GO AND SELL ALL YOU POSSESS

Consider the rich young ruler who came to Jesus and asked, "What shall I do to inherit eternal life?" (Mark 10:17). This young businessman lived to acquire and admire the things of this world. Material possessions, and the prestige and power that accompanied them, were the driving force of his life. Yet despite all his money and popularity, they did not satisfy the deepest cravings of his heart. His restlessness and emptiness drove him to seek Jesus.

As Jesus looked within this man's unconverted heart, He saw the root sin of covetousness—the consuming desire for the things of this world. So Jesus said, "Go and sell all you possess and give to the poor, and you will have treasure in heaven; and come, follow Me" (Mark 10:21). Jesus called this young man to renounce his love affair with this world so that a new love affair with God could begin.

Like so many today, the rich young ruler's desire for the world was so strong he was unwilling to forsake it. He refused to let the world go from his heart, and love for God could not take root.

A LOVE-HATE RELATIONSHIP

On another occasion, Jesus perceived that many among the crowd who followed Him were merely jumping on the bandwagon of His popularity. So He said to them, "If anyone comes to Me, and does not hate his own father and mother and wife and children and brothers and sisters, yes, and even his own life, he cannot be My disciple" (Luke 14:26).

Jesus called for these halfhearted followers to renounce all loyalties to their closest relationships in order to establish Him as their chief love. He said if anyone truly loved Him, his allegiance to his own family would appear to be as hate by comparison. Jesus is a jealous Master who will not settle for second place in any life.

Jesus went on to say, "No one of you can be My disciple who does not give up all his own possessions" (Luke 14:33). In essence, we cannot follow Him unless we transfer all that we own to Him. We must give up all claims to what we possess if we are to be His disciples. Jesus demands our absolute, unconditional surrender. He declares that no one can hold on to this world and follow Him.

This does not mean that we must live a life of poverty to enter the kingdom of God. But it does mean that we cannot cling to our earthly possessions if we are to embrace Christ. Anything that comes between Christ and us must go. All that we own must be acknowledged as belonging to God.

A LIFE-OR-DEATH DEVOTION

At another time, Jesus said, "If anyone wishes to come after Me, let him deny himself, and take up his cross, and follow Me" (Matthew 16:24). This is an invitation to total commitment to Christ. Cross-bearing pictures a convicted criminal carrying his cross from the judge's courtroom through the streets of the city to the place of public execution. Thus, Jesus is calling for the unreserved surrender of our life if we would follow Him.

Adding the knockout punch, Jesus said, "For whoever wishes to save his life shall lose it; but whoever loses his life for My sake shall find it. For what will a man be profited, if he gains the whole world, and forfeits his soul? Or what will a man give in exchange for his soul?" (Matthew 16:25–26). The answers to these rhetorical questions are blatantly obvious. Living for this world will result in losing one's soul eternally and forfeiting eternal life. If one is to be saved, he must renounce his pursuit of this world to embrace Christ.

FAME AND FORTUNE

C. T. Studd, a cricket player in England in the nineteenth century, became a world-famous sports personality as he starred as the captain of his Eton team.

But the Lord had different plans for him. While attending Cambridge University, Studd heard the great evangelist D. L. Moody preach and was wondrously converted. Immediately, he began spending hours seeking to convert his teammates.

Soon Studd sensed God's call to full-time ministry and offered himself to Hudson Taylor for missionary work in China. While in

China, he received word that he had inherited a vast amount of money from his privileged family. Immediately Studd returned to his native homeland to receive his inheritance. What would he do now? Stay in England and enjoy a life of luxury? Return to the popularity and stardom of the cricket field? Retire from the mission field?

To the astonishment of a watching world, young Studd gave away the entire inheritance to the work of God's kingdom—within twenty-four hours! As one who had died to the world, C. T. Studd released his money and continued in his faithful service for God.

Such is the reality of true conversion to Christ. Although we may never inherit a vast fortune, nor feel led to give away all that we have, nevertheless those who have experienced the life-changing power of the new birth live not for this world, but for the world to come.

FRIENDSHIP WITH THE WORLD

Friendship with this world results in enmity toward God. The Bible says, "You adulteresses, do you not know that friendship with the world is hostility toward God? Therefore whoever wishes to be a friend of the world makes himself an enemy of God" (James 4:4). No one can love this world and be a friend of God. Love for one mandates a rejection of the other. If we live for this world, we declare ourselves the enemy of God, something that would never be true of a genuine believer.

Turned one way, two magnets pull toward each other. If you flip one magnet over, however, the two now repel. So it is with salvation. The pull of our hearts toward the world is reversed when we are born again by the Spirit of God. Our new heart is now repelled by the world it once loved and is drawn toward Christ.

Some who profess Christ remain absorbed with the things of this world. Such people, though outwardly religious, are inwardly lost. Worldly minded people may give substantially to the church, may serve on church boards, may even be thrust into key leadership positions, but still not know Christ. A self-indulgent lifestyle that feeds off the world's approval, applause, and possessions rather than love for God has yet to truly believe in Christ.

A PERPETUAL BATTLE

This does not mean we have no recurring struggle with the world. Temptation is real. The allure of the world is seductive. And it continues to entice our hearts.

As I look back over my life, one of the greatest battles with the world took place while I was in seminary. Living in upscale, affluent Dallas was not easy for a struggling student. During that time, I wrote small magazines with the Dallas Cowboys and Texas Rangers to support myself financially.

Unexpectedly, I had the opportunity to make lots of money with these publications, and associating with the National Football League and Major League Baseball was a whole lot more fun than memorizing Hebrew vocabulary and parsing Greek verbs. My heart was pulled in two directions as the world was seeking to gain a foothold in my heart.

But by the grace of God, I was able to resist the more than subtle temptation to pursue the world. God would not let go of me. He strengthened my heart and enabled me to remain true to His calling upon my life. But not without a fight.

THE POLLUTION OF THE WORLD

John describes the major forces that Satan uses to drive the world system. Here's what makes the world go round:

> For all that is in the world, the lust of the flesh and the lust of the eyes and the boastful pride of life, is not from the Father, but is from the world. (1 John 2:16)

Lust and pride are deeply embedded within the lost souls of those held captive by this evil world system. These deadly forces draw a man or woman away from God and prevent a genuine con-version, no matter how religious the person may be. Satan sets before our eyes the things of the world to cause our flesh to lust after them and to stimulate the boastful pride of life. He keeps his captives living for the things of the world, and they remain self-deceived about their spiritual state.

As long as lust and pride rule one's life, there can be no self-denial, no repentance, no saving faith. Only the life-changing power of the new birth can radically alter one's life, transforming love for this world into love for Christ. And, of course, none of these things can be self-generated but are produced exclusively by a true work of grace within our hearts.

THE WORLD IS SELF-DESTRUCTING

Although outwardly alluring, this world system is actually self-destructing and headed for God's final judgment. Tragically, all unbe-lievers will have a part in this end-time, cataclysmic judgment.

> And the world is passing away, and also its lusts; but the one who does the will of God lives forever. (1 John 2:17)

This evil world system is "passing away"; it is in the process of dis-integrating. It is not becoming better and better but is actually crum-bling away, self-destructing, and unraveling. Living for this world is like rearranging the deck furniture on the *Titanic*. It is a preoccupation with things that are perishing. This world is doomed, headed for a watery grave below, and all who are living for this world will perish with it.

The warning is clear: abandon ship before it's too late! This world has a gaping hole and is taking water quickly. She is going down. The world has struck the iceberg of God's judgment and will submerge all on board with it. There is only one way to be saved: believe upon Jesus Christ, not merely with an intellectual assent to the historical facts of the life of Christ, but with a decisive step of faith that makes total surrender to Christ.

This decisive break with the world is one of the clearest evidences that one is born again. The one who is genuinely converted will no longer be preoccupied with the triviality of this present age, but will pursue the eternal treasures of the kingdom of God. Certainly, there will be momentary times and isolated seasons when a child of God will yield to the seductive lure of the world. But on the whole, the one who is born of God will give clear evidence of his salvation by setting his mind on things above and not on things of the earth (Colossians 3:2).

BLESSED ASSURANCE: NEW LOVE

Would you like to know for sure if you are a Christian? Would you like to have the assurance of your salvation? Do you want to know with certainty that you will escape the coming final judgment of this world? Then search your heart and answer these questions:

- Is loving Christ your greatest priority?
- Is knowing God your greatest treasure?
- Does the world no longer appeal to you like it once did?
- Has your love for God now replaced love for the world?
- Do you long for the world to come?

If you can answer yes to these questions, a positive assurance of salvation will be yours. We are saved by faith alone in Christ alone, but genuine saving faith will always make its presence known in a changed life. If you are saved, you will no longer love, nor live for, this world that is passing away. Instead you will love God supremely.

If you cannot give positive answers to these questions, then you need to reexamine the authenticity of your faith. Perhaps you have only gone through the empty motions of religious activity and have never actually received Christ. If so, I urge you to believe on Him today. Give up on this world for the unseen world to come. Replace love for this world with love for God.

Step out in faith now.

SEEING

IS BELIEVING

Vital Sign #6: Comprehension of the Truth

1 JOHN 2:18–27; 4:1–6

The gospel is light, but only the Spirit can give sight.

A. W. Tozer

On a recent vacation, my family and I were driving together down the highway when my daughter began to read out loud the words on the back of a large truck in front of us. Squinting to focus his eyes, our seven-year-old son John blurted out in disbelief, "You can't see those letters."

"Oh yes, I can," my daughter confidently replied, reading the sign again.

He still refused to believe that his sister could read the words. Leaning forward in his seat, John squinted again and tried to read the letters, but to no avail. A terrific reader, he simply could not see the sign well enough to read it.

Then it dawned on me my wife: unknown to us our son was near-sighted. All the while believing he could see, in actuality he couldn't.

OPEN MY EYES, LORD

So it is with many people who claim to be Christians. Those who are genuinely converted to Christ can see; others who merely say they are saved but are not cannot see.

True believers can see God's truth because they have been enlightened by the Holy Spirit. But those who assume they are Christians when they are not are unable to see the light of the gospel when it is presented to them. Thinking they see, they are actually spiritually blind.

Regeneration is an eye-opening experience. By the illuminating ministry of the Holy Spirit, those who are born again are supernaturally enabled to comprehend the truth about the divine person, earthly mission, and saving work of Jesus Christ. It is the Spirit who enlightens all true believers—John calls it "the anointing"—and teaches them the essential, nonnegotiable truth about Christ.

SEEING THROUGH IT

Such spiritual discernment was critically important in John's day because the false teachers we mentioned previously—the gnostics—were spreading their damnable lies in the church. After a season of deception, these false teachers were withdrawing from the fellowship, having established a beachhead within the congregation, and were pulling away many with them.

At the heart of their false teaching was a warped view of Christ's deity and His humanity. For the gnostics, Christ was neither fully God nor fully man. He was more of a ghost than God, more of a phantom than man. The effect of this was presenting "another Christ" who could not die for our sins upon the cross. Those who accepted this false doctrine were buying into the devil's lies and were in danger of being eternally damned.

John writes that those who are truly saved would see clearly the truth about Christ and see through the deception of the false teachers. Those who know Christ understand the true nature of His deity and death. It is this God-given enlightenment that provides assurance of salvation. Seeing is believing.

But those who are religious yet unconverted are without the God-given spiritual vision to see who Jesus is and why He came. Thus, they are deceived and will be damned if they do not repent and believe in Christ now.

A GREAT AND PRESENT DANGER

John warns us of false teachers who were already infiltrating the church and spreading their deadly doctrine.

> Children, it is the last hour; and just as you heard that antichrist is coming, even now many antichrists have appeared; from this we know that it is the last hour. (1 John 2:18)

From God's perspective, the entire period between the first and second comings of Christ is "the last hour." This time span is the final scene in redemptive history, climaxing in Christ's glorious return (1 John 2:28; 3:2–3). Yet as the time of the end approaches, there will be a great proliferation of evil. At the consumation of this age, a malicious man called the antichrist will rise to power and dominate the world with his evil reign of terror (2 Thessalonians 2:3–12).

Stand guard, says John, because until then, many antichrists, or false prophets, will arise within the church throughout this age. In every generation, many false teachers will distort the person and work of Jesus Christ. These antichrists are Satan's inside plants to sow and spread their damnable lies within the church, either through open and blatant opposition of Christ, or by subtle, deceptive attempts to defile the truth about Christ. It is the latter of these that is most deadly.

Currently, these false prophets occupy pulpits, teach in colleges, oversee seminaries, lead denominations, serve on church pastoral staffs, lead seminars, hold conferences, write books, host television programs, appear on the radio, and record music albums. Assuming multiple facades, these unholy hypocrites are a real and present danger to the church.

Jesus Himself warned it would be so when He said, "False Christs and false prophets will arise, and will show signs and wonders, in order, if possible, to lead the elect astray" (Mark 13:22). Armed with miracle-working power from Satan, these teachers will exercise extraordinary influence, so much so that were it not for the persevering ministry of the Holy Spirit in true believers, even the elect would be led astray.

NOT ONE OF US

John says these antichrists rise up quickly within the church and then fade off the scene just as fast.

> They went out from us, but they were not really of us; for if they had been of us, they would have remained with us; but they went out, so that it would be shown that they all are not of us. (1 John 2:19)

As these dispensers of damnable doctrine establish a foothold within the church, they will draw to themselves those who are not genuinely converted to Christ. Eventually they will exit the fellowship, defecting to go their own way, and draw out of the church the gullible, unsaved followers who superficially identify with Christ.

The defection of these false prophets only serves to reveal their true colors. Truth is, the gospel seed fell on shallow ground in their lives, never truly taking root. If these false leaders and their duped disciples were truly saved, they would have continued in the fellowship with the true believers. If someone departs from the church to follow false doctrine, you can be sure he or she was never a true believer.

In His sovereignty, God allows apostasy as one way of purging the church. The Head of the church allows false teachers to rise up within the church to draw away bogus believers, thus cleansing and purifying the bride of Christ.

A MOUTHPIECE OF SATAN

Such was the case with Jonestown, one of the most incredible tragedies of our lifetime. If ever there was an illustration of a false prophet who abandoned the faith, left the church, and drew with him other apparent believers, it was Jim Jones. Once identified with evangelical Christianity,

Jones departed to form his own false religion at the People's Temple in San Francisco.

Although giving many outward appearances of being a true spiritual leader, he nevertheless was a mouthpiece for Satan. This self-styled false prophet fooled people into believing that he represented God and Christ. So persuasive was this antichrist that he drew nearly one thousand people with him to Guyana, South America. And his followers, believing that they were receiving the truth of God, drank poison under the assumption that they were going to heaven. But they are now in hell.

The greatest tragedy of Jonestown is not that nearly one thousand people died. Everyone will one day die. The tragedy is that they died and went to hell, all the while believing they were serving God and on their way to heaven.

Not all false prophets are as blatantly obvious as Jim Jones. They come in all types of packages; most are very spiritual sounding, subtle, and alluring. However, their hearts are always the same. They peddle the lies of the devil and turn people away from the truth, pulling away many from Bible-believing churches where the truth is preached.

BELIEVER'S LIE DETECTOR

How can believers detect false teachers within the church and escape undefiled? God has provided an "early warning system" for all believers—the Holy Spirit.

> But you have an anointing from the Holy One, and you all
> know. I have not written to you because you do not know the
> truth, but because you do know it, and because no lie is of the
> truth (1 John 2:20–21).

All true Christians have an anointing from God that gives them penetrating insight into the truth. This anointing is the ministry of God the Holy Spirit in the life of every genuine believer, revealing the truth of Scripture, as well as protecting him from doctrinal error. At our conversion, Jesus Christ baptized us with the Holy Spirit, "the Spirit of truth" (John 14:17; 15:26; 16:13), who gives us the true knowledge of the essentials of the faith, as well as protects us from the hellish heresies of these antichrists.

On the eve of His crucifixion, Jesus promised to send to every believer a divine Teacher when He said, "But the Helper, the Holy Spirit, whom the Father will send in My name, He will teach you all things, and bring to your remembrance all that I said to you" (John 14:26). This was a guarantee that what the apostles recorded as Scripture is, in fact, the very Word of God. But we can also gain great comfort because this same Holy Spirit who inspired the apostles to remember all of Jesus' words is the very One who lives within us and guides us into a right understanding of the truth (John 14:16–17).

No real believer will fall into apostasy, John says, because the Holy Spirit is our built-in lie detector. We have a spiritual radar that detects the infiltration of the devil's subversive attacks. What the antichrists are peddling, we are not buying.

WHO IS THE LIAR?

How can we identify these false teachers? What do they look like? What do they sound like? John doesn't leave us to speculate.

> Who is the liar but the one who denies that Jesus is the Christ? This is the antichrist, the one who denies the Father and the Son. Whoever denies the Son does not have the Father; the one who confesses the Son has the Father also. (1 John 2:22–23)

Ultimately, the one who pushes Satan's lies is anyone who denies that Jesus Christ is who He claimed to be. With subtle perversion, these deceptive teachers deny that Jesus is God in human flesh who came to be the Savior of the world. Why must we believe that Jesus is

God in human flesh? Christ had to be who He was (God in human flesh) in order to do what He did (die a death of infinite value). Jesus had to be infinite, eternal God in order to die an infinite, eternal death that will provide an infinite, eternal salvation.

These antichrists, John warns, deny that a holy, just God sent His Son to be the only solution for man's sin problem. They deny the unique relationship between the Father and the Son as equals. Thus, they deny that the Son is the only way to the Father.

John reminds us that salvation is a package deal. One cannot have the Father without having the Son and vice versa. Deny the Son, deny the Father. Reject the Son, reject the Father. But confess the Son, possess the Father. The two are inseparably bound together. Jesus said, "I and the Father are one" (John 10:30).

TRUE BELIEVERS WILL REMAIN

Lest there be any uncertainty, John reiterates that true believers will continue in the truth and never apostatize.

> As for you, let that abide in you which you heard from the beginning. If what you heard from the beginning abides in you, you also will abide in the Son and in the Father. This is the promise which He Himself made to us: eternal life. These things I have written to you concerning those who are trying to deceive you. (1 John 2:24–26)

Like a stake driven into the ground, God's truth about the person and work of Jesus Christ will always remain in those who are truly saved. From the beginning of his Christian experience, the genuine believer will hold tenaciously to the essential truths of the gospel and endure faithfully in sound doctrine until the end. This is an extraordinary claim! John is saying, "If the gospel abides in you, you will remain in the Son and the Father, as well as in their truth."

Jesus said the same: "If you continue in My word, then you are

truly disciples of Mine" (John 8:31). That is to say, all true believers
will continue in their understanding of and obedience to God's Word.
Perseverance in the truth is the mark of every authentic believer. Paul
confirms this by identifying those who are redeemed and reconciled
in Christ as those who "continue in the faith firmly established and
steadfast, and not moved away from the hope of the gospel" (Colossians 1:23).

So, although these false teachers attempt to deceive us by trying to
reroute the way to heaven, the truth is, we won't fall for it. Referring
to the God-given discernment of His sheep, Jesus said, "A stranger
they simply will not follow, but will flee from him, because they do
not know the voice of strangers" (John 10:5). Instead of succumbing
to the allure of these frauds, we will remain firm in our attachment to
the truth as we follow Christ.

ABIDE IN HIM, ABIDE

Abiding is a twofold partnership. As a result of God's abiding in us, we
now abide in Him.

> As for you, the anointing which you received from Him
> abides in you, and you have no need for anyone to teach you;
> but as His anointing teaches you about all things, and is true
> and is not a lie, and just as it has taught you, you abide in
> Him. (1 John 2:27)

John reminds us that all true believers will remain steadfast in the
truth because the Holy Spirit will continue His work in us—regardless of our frailties. We cannot turn back because the Holy Spirit will
not turn His back on us. We will persevere in the truth because the
Holy Spirit shall persevere in us. Consequently, we have no need for
any so-called teacher to teach us anything new that is contrary to
God's Word. If it's new, it's not true!

Our primary responsibility is, simply stated, to "abide in Him."

Because Christ, by His Spirit within us, is sufficient to protect and preserve us, let us remain steadfast in our reliance upon Him, resting in His grace and receiving from Him all we need to press on faithfully to the end. As we abide in Him, His abiding in us is more fully experienced by our hearts.

TEST THE SPIRITS

John continues this subject of false prophets in 1 John 4:1–6 as he enlarges upon the elementary principles he set out in chapter 2.

> Beloved, do not believe every spirit, but test the spirits to see whether they are from God, because many false prophets have gone out into the world. (1 John 4:1)

Because of the danger these false prophets present to the church—a danger that will not go away—John admonishes us to "test the spirits" since not every spirit is from God. There are two opposing sides in the spiritual warfare for the minds of men. There is the Holy Spirit who is from God, and there are demon spirits who are from Satan. Therefore we must test and discern the spirits because not everything spiritual is from God. Behind every false prophet is a demon spirit who passes off the devil's lies. Whether knowingly or not, every false prophet who denies the full deity and full humanity of Christ, as well as distorts the sufficiency of His sacrifice for our sins, is energized and empowered by a demon spirit, "the spirit of error" (4:6).

Lest we be caught off guard, Scripture clearly warns that this tidal wave of false doctrine spawned by false teachers will always batter the church. Paul writes, "But the Spirit explicitly says that in later times some will fall away from the faith, paying attention to deceitful spirits and doctrines of demons" (1 Timothy 4:1). As the last days of the later times approach, such lies from demon-inspired false teachers will only increase.

Surely such days are here! All around us, many false teachers are leading the false believers down the broad path headed to destruction (Matthew 7:13, 15–20). And as the time for the end approaches, their numbers will only escalate.

WHO IS JESUS CHRIST?

How can we discern who these false teachers are? How may we identify them?

> By this you know the Spirit of God: every spirit that confesses that Jesus Christ has come in the flesh is from God; and every spirit that does not confess Jesus is not from God. (1 John 4:2–3)

Beware, John says, because phony prophets will freely use the name of Jesus. They will talk about Him, expound upon His ethic, emphasize His love, and even reference His death, burial, and resurrection. But they will not believe what the Bible so clearly teaches about why He came and what He did. Although they speak His name and even use biblical terms, they assign deadly interpretations to these truths, and, in so doing, twist the Scriptures.

Let us understand, the primary point of apostasy for every false teacher is distorting the person and work of Christ. They will say Jesus is a god, denying His full deity, or say he is an angel, or the brother of the devil, or some other distorted concoction, denying His humanity. In addition, they will teach a works salvation, denying that salvation is by grace alone through faith alone in Christ alone. They will add human works such as baptism, church membership, or some other religious activity to the simplicity of faith in the saving work of Jesus Christ upon the Cross.

This is the crux of the crisis, the apex of the apostasy, the heart of the heresy—*who is Jesus, why did He come,* and *what did He accomplish?* To depart from sound teaching regarding Christ is to embark upon a path that leads to eternal hell.

GREATER IS HE

To bolster our faith and increase our confidence in the midst of this spiritual battle, John reminds us that the Holy Spirit of truth within us is far greater than the demon spirits of error in the world.

> You are from God, little children, and have overcome them; because greater is He who is in you than he who is in the world. (1 John 4:4)

As Spirit-indwelt believers, we have overcome all the lies, deceptions, and heresies of Satan because the Holy Spirit is greater in teaching the truth than demon spirits are in destroying and denying it. With God-given discernment, true believers see through the scheming lies and remain anchored in the truth.

Christ, the greatest Teacher of all, made this abundantly clear when He told His disciples about "another Helper...the Spirit of truth, whom the world cannot receive" (John 14:16–17). The world does not know the truth because it does not have the Spirit of truth. As the light always overpowers and extinguishes the darkness, so the Spirit of truth, the Holy Spirit, always overcomes the spirit of error who confuses and corrupts the world.

POPULAR BUT POLLUTED

John warns us that these false prophets will be very popular with the world.

> They are from the world; therefore they speak as from the world, and the world listens to them. (1 John 4:5)

Make no mistake about it, these charlatans are from the world. They are a part of "the system" that is hostile toward God, and they rebel against His Word (1 John 2:15–16). And they have invaded the church, bringing with them their worldly philosophy.

Because they are from the world, they are absorbed with all that is in the world, "the lust of the flesh and the lust of the eyes and the boastful pride of life" (1 John 2:16). These hell-bound hucksters are absorbed with pride, power, prestige, and popularity. Like the world around them, they are self-centered, self-righteous, self-willed, self-absorbed, self-flattering, self-promoting. They are the epitome of the system, "selling" religion to advance themselves at the expense of others.

Using the Bible as a camouflage, they teach and preach a message "from the world." They repackage the world's lies, dressed up in religious jargon as though it were from God. But it is from hell. They may change the label on the bottle, but it's still the same old poison on the inside.

The unbelieving world, especially unbelievers in the church, drink in and eat up what they say. The world listens to them because these polluted prophets are on the world's wavelength. They speak the world's language and say what the world wants to hear. Thus, they are loved and accepted by the world.

Far from being persecuted by the world, which is the mark of the true prophet (Matthew 5:10–12), these satanic mouthpieces are very popular with the world. They are applauded as examples of virtue and lauded for their religiosity. But if they ever stopped corrupting and compromising God's truth, they would be deserted by the world in a heartbeat. If they ever preached repentance and judgment, self-denial and suffering, obedience and Lordship, the world would tune them out for another ear tickler.

AN EAR FOR TRUTH

True believers follow true teachers of the Word, John concludes. False believers follow false teachers.

> We are from God; he who knows God listens to us; he who is not from God does not listen to us. By this we know the spirit of truth and the spirit of error. (1 John 4:6)

When false Christians hear a true man of God preach the truth of God's Word, they refuse to hear it. They will either attack the one bringing the truth or withdraw from the fellowship and find a teacher "in accordance to their own desires" (2 Timothy 4:3).

As I noted earlier, God allows heresy in the church to serve as a magnet to draw away false disciples from the church. Ironically, God uses error in the church to separate the chaff from the wheat. The presence of polluted pastors and lying leaders serves to reveal who is unconverted in the church. Such men are allowed by God to draw ungodly people to themselves and, eventually, out of the church as a part of God's purging the bride of Christ.

ARE YOU OF THE TRUTH?

All who are truly saved are rooted and grounded in the truth. The certainty of salvation belongs to those who experience the illumination and enlightenment of the Holy Spirit, who enables us to discern spiritual truth from what is false. It is the anointing that produces the assurance.

Let me ask you, can you discern between divine truth and error? Do you sense the ministry of God's resident truth-teacher, the Holy Spirit, within you? Are you established in sound doctrine?

Do you detect the clever presentations of the cults and other false religious groups? Can you distinguish between God's truth and Satan's lies?

Salvation is an eye-opening experience. If the grace of God has truly come into your life, then you will know the truth. Sight produces certainty; illumination confirms conversion.

Because seeing is believing.

BE RIGHT OR BE LEFT!

Vital Sign #7: Conformity to Christlikeness

1 JOHN 2:28–3:10

If Christ justifies you He will sanctify you!
He will not save you and leave you in your sins.

Robert Murray M'Cheyne

lexander the Great was infuriated! The infamous ruler was holding court in the Babylonian palace of Nebuchadnezzar, seated upon his great golden throne, surrounded with hundreds of soldiers in full-dressed regalia. One by one, the sergeant at arms ushered before Alexander the arrested citizens, read their crimes, and anxiously awaited his verdict.

After hearing each case, Alexander the Great, the most powerful man in the world, would announce the sentence. When this potentate spoke, there was no reversing his decision, no appealing to a higher court, no second chance. His royal decree was final.

On this day, a blond-haired, blue-eyed, seventeen-year-old soldier was brought before Alexander. The sergeant at arms read aloud how he had fled battle in the face of the enemy and been caught hiding in a cave. A crime of such cowardly conduct would normally infuriate the emperor, but the innocence on the young boy's face began to evoke sympathy from Alexander's heart.

As the king beheld this young soldier, he inquired, "Son, what is your name?" All spectators in the room held their breath as the boy replied, "Alexander, sir."

"What did you say?"

"Alexander, sir," the boy said, standing at military attention.

Turning scarlet, the king asked one more time, "What is your name?"

Stammering in fear the boy said, "Al...Alex...Alexander, sir."

Emerging from his throne, the king grabbed the young soldier by his tunic, lifted him in the air, stared him in the face, then threw him to the ground and said, "Soldier, change your conduct, or change your name."

A CHANGED LIFE

So it is with everyone who bears the name of Christ. If we bear His name, then our life and conduct must be in conformity with His holy character. That's what it means to be a Christian and to adopt His name. A Christian is a follower of Christ or one who imitates Christ. A Christian is a mimic of Christ. If we take His name, then we must live a life that is consistent with Christ's holy character.

But unfortunately, not everyone who claims to be a Christian lives like Him. It is to this one that Christ says, in essence, "Change your conduct, or change your name."

In the life of every true Christian, there will be the pursuit of Christlikeness. A Christian is one who knows Christ, follows Christ, and is becoming like Christ. His life bears a distinct resemblance to the One whose name he bears. This pursuit of holiness, called sanctification, is the lifelong process of the true believer in which he experiences a decreasing pattern of sin and an increasing practice of righteousness. While we never become sinless, we do sin less. Sin remains in us, but sin no longer reigns in us. The more we pursue and practice holiness, the less we sin.

THE KEY WORD: RIGHTEOUSNESS

The key word that identifies this vital sign is *righteousness*. Rich in meaning, this word, the Greek *dikaiosune*, conveys the idea of conformity to a standard, or conformity to the claims of a higher authority. Righteousness means that a believer will live in conformity to God's character, claims, and commands as revealed in Jesus Christ and God's Word.

Since God Himself is the standard, living a righteous life means to live a godly life. Righteousness is the pursuit of holiness or a life being brought into conformity with Christlikeness. All true believers will practice righteousness (1 John 2:29; 3:7, 10). All who do not, no matter what they may claim, are self-deceived, counterfeit Christians.

It is the practice of righteousness in our daily lives that brings the assurance of our salvation. If we see righteousness being produced in our lives, then we can be certain that we belong to Christ.

Do you see evidences of Christlikeness in your life? Are you purifying yourself as He is pure? Is your life distinctive? Are your words clean? Are your thoughts godly? Are your deeds righteous?

For any true believer, one of the most powerful motivations to live righteously is the sure hope of Christ's return. This blessed hope will purify us from the defilements of this evil world. Jesus will return for His own, and all who belong to Him will be easily recognizable. At His appearing, those who are practicing righteousness will be caught up into the air and taken to heaven with Him. Because He is coming to take us out of this world, we will have a decreasing desire to be a part of the world.

READY OR NOT?

John tells us that since Jesus is returning, we need to remain faithful to Him. His sure return is the impetus for us to grow in likeness to Him.

> Now, little children, abide in Him, so that when He appears, we may have confidence and not shrink away from Him in shame at His coming. (1 John 2:28)

At the time of Christ's return, there will be two groups of people in the church. One group will be abiding in Christ—the true Christians.

The other group, although they will claim a relationship to Christ, will not be abiding in Him. These are false believers. It is those who are abiding in Him who will rejoice at His coming. These are the genuine believers who abide in Him. But when He appears, those unsaved who are not abiding in Christ will be stricken with terrible grief. In that day, many who profess to know Christ but do not possess Him will be horrified to face the consequences.

"Abiding in Christ," John says, is evidence that salvation is real. That means a true believer will remain in close relationship with Christ, rely upon His grace, and persevere in faithfulness to Him. To abide in Christ means that one has received Christ and is resting in His grace, relying upon His power, and remaining in close fellowship with Him. As a branch abides in the vine, so these believers rely upon Christ and remain closely connected to Him. Although they may give the outward appearance of starting well, counterfeit believers will eventually fall away and return to their previous worldliness. The abiding produces the assurance.

At the time of Christ's return, there will be a separation of true believers from make-believers. Those who genuinely know Christ will be caught up to meet the Lord in the air (1 Thessalonians 4:17). But those who merely give lip service to knowing Christ will be passed over to face the wrath of God in the Tribulation. At the Rapture of the church, the sheep will be taken, and the goats left behind.

RECOGNIZING THE REDEEMED

Lest any of us be deceived over the state of our souls, John says it is the one who is practicing righteousness who is born again.

> If you know that He is righteous, you know that everyone also who practices righteousness is born of Him. (1 John 2:29)

How can one know that he or she is truly saved? Not by being in church or by being involved in religious activities. Rather, John says a righteous life is what gives the assurance of salvation. "The one who practices righteousness is born of Him," he writes. It is the one who is growing in Christlikeness who truly knows Christ. An un-Christlike Christian is a contradiction in terms.

A family resemblance is found in every family, and God's family is no exception. Just as children take on the likeness of their parents, so God's children bear a resemblance to the One who begot them, Jesus Christ. Those who are truly born again will display a Christlike righteousness in their lives just as He who begot them is righteous.

What does it mean that Jesus is righteous? Simply this, that He alone perfectly conforms to the holiness of God. At His first coming, Jesus lived a perfect, righteous life, "holy, innocent, undefiled, separated from sinners" (Hebrews 7:26). He "committed no sin, nor was any deceit found in His mouth" (1 Peter 2:22). As "the Holy and Righteous One" (Acts 3:14), He "knew no sin" (2 Corinthians 5:21). He was "tempted in all things as we are, yet without sin" (Hebrews 4:15).

Through the miracle of the new birth, Christ's righteous nature is implanted within us and we will begin to display His righteous character. Righteous living is the result of receiving a new, righteous nature through the new birth.

When Christ returns, He will summon all those who resemble Him. We will be easy to detect. Those who are practicing righteousness as He Himself is righteous will be transported to heaven.

At His coming, there will be no second chance to get right with God. In the twinkling of an eye—in a split second—one will be taken, the other will be left. So we need to be absolutely sure that we belong to Him. We must be certain that we are marching in allegiance under the bloodstained banner of our King, Jesus Christ.

If you are to have the assurance of your salvation, you must ask yourself: Do I see the practical righteousness of Jesus Christ manifested in my life? Am I in the process of being conformed to His holy standard? Even though sin may seem frequent, am I, nevertheless, making progress toward the goal of Christlikeness? And when Jesus arrives on the scene, will He recognize me as bearing the family image?

AN ENIGMA TO THE WORLD

Prepare yourself—the more you become like Christ, the less the world will understand you.

> See how great a love the Father has bestowed on us, that we should be called children of God; and such we are. For this reason the world does not know us, because it did not know Him. (1 John 3:1)

A righteous life will stand out in this world. In fact, the genuine believer will be an enigma to a lost and dying world. Those who are of the world will no more understand him than they understood Christ Himself.

The Christian life is so supernaturally empowered that it cannot be explained by a watching world. They cannot comprehend that it is God at work within us, radically transforming our lives. Although the world will reject us, we are loved by the Father and find in Him the strength and comfort we need to live victoriously during our short stay on this earth.

The more we bask in the Father's love, the more the world will not know us. Before our conversion, the world knew us quite well because we were on the world's wavelength, operating like those in the world. But after our new birth, we display a new lifestyle that is antithetical to the world's standards. That's why the world cannot understand us.

Herein is assurance of your salvation. If the world doesn't understand you, be assured that you are known by God. So we should stop trying to be popular with the world. Acceptance by the world would cause the assurance of our salvation to waver.

God forbid that we should ever desire to become like the world.

May we never seek to embrace its value system, follow its choices, or adopt its wisdom. Every true child of God will be different and distinct from the world and, therefore, misunderstood by it.

OUR GLORIOUS FUTURE

Everyone who is born again is immediately made a member of God's family and given a glorious future, climaxing when Christ returns.

> Beloved, now we are children of God, and it has not appeared as yet what we shall be. We know that when He appears, we will be like Him, because we will see Him just as He is. (1 John 3:2)

We can be certain that we are children of God by living a righteous life. However, the future has not yet been fully revealed to us. All we know, and all we need to know, is that when Christ appears, we will be made like Him. In that glorious day, we will be perfectly conformed to the image of Christ.

Michelangelo said that in every block of stone he saw an angel waiting to be unveiled. In like fashion, there is within every believer the pattern of Christlikeness that God is working to produce and will be brought to completion when Jesus returns. We are like a building undergoing extensive renovation. God is tearing down and removing certain aspects of our lives that do not conform to Christlikeness while He is also building godliness in us.

When Jesus comes back, God will fully complete the renovation. At the time of His appearing, wherever we are in this process of growing into Christlikeness, God will complete whatever is lacking. When you stand before Him, you will be like Him perfectly. Paul writes, "For I am confident of this very thing, that He who began a good work in you will perfect it until the day of Christ Jesus" (Philippians 1:6).

Essentially, we will undergo a twofold change. First, our physical bodies will be made like Christ's glorified resurrection body. "The

Lord Jesus Christ…will transform the body of our humble state into conformity with the body of His glory" (Philippians 3:20–21). Second, our inner being will be made perfectly holy. In that moment God will eradicate our sin nature, and we will be liberated to do only that which is righteous and pure. In heaven, we will never again struggle with an evil thought nor ever say a disparaging word. We will no longer be lured into sin or face the slightest temptation.

We will undergo this dramatic transformation because "we shall see Him just as He is" (1 John 3:2). We must be made like Him in order to see Him. We must become glorified if we are to see the glorified Lord. In our mortal flesh, we could not look upon Christ and live. That's why people fell at His feet as though dead when they caught a mere glimpse of His glory. If we are to see Him, we must be made like Him.

A HOPE THAT PURIFIES

Our glorious future will have a profound effect on our daily behavior. It is unthinkable that such a blessed hope would not radically alter the way we live today.

> And everyone who has this hope fixed on Him purifies himself, just as He is pure. (1 John 3:3)

When the Bible speaks of hope, it refers to something in the future that is certain. This word is loaded with punch, unlike its meaning today, which conveys a wishful desire that may or may not be fulfilled. But in the Bible, hope is a belief in an absolute, fixed certainty about the future, a confident assurance about tomorrow.

As we grasp the hope of Christ's return, it will surely grip our hearts. It will purify us and set us apart from this evil world. The reality of Christ's return makes a difference in our behavior. Since we will be completely like Christ in the future, we are exhorted to live like Him today.

GUESS WHO'S COMING?

Suppose I came to you and said, "Would you mind if Billy Graham stayed at your house tonight?" I'm sure you would be overjoyed to have the famed Dr. Graham as your houseguest. And if you really believed he was coming to spend the night with you, you would begin cleaning your house so it would be extra presentable.

You might repair a few broken objects or paint over some dirty spots on the wall. Certainly you would clean up the bedroom in which he would be staying and change the sheets. You might even put out a Bible next to his bed.

But whether Dr. Graham ever comes to your house is insignificant compared to the fact that Jesus Christ is returning to this planet for His own. And if we truly believe He is coming back, we will begin cleaning up our lives today.

Some of us need to scour the walls of our hearts. Others of us need to scrub the floors of our inner thoughts. Still others need to put some garbage in the trash can. Some things need to be rearranged, other things removed. But all of us need to purify ourselves as He is pure.

Such righteous living gives clear evidence that we have been born again.

CALLING SIN WHAT IT IS

Lest there be any misunderstanding about what we are to put away, John explains what sin really is. It is a lawlessness or open rebellion against God. And no Christian, he says, will live in an unbroken pattern of moral anarchy.

> Everyone who practices sin also practices lawlessness; and sin is lawlessness. (1 John 3:4)

Lawlessness, or *anomia,* means "living as if there is no law." It pictures one who conducts his life without God's moral standard, living however he pleases, having no regard for what God says. He may claim to know God, but he lives as if there is no God. Such a person is obviously not a Christian.

No one who is genuinely converted to Christ is going to live in ongoing, open rebellion against God's Word. The true Christian has submitted his or her life to the authority of God's Word. Divine law becomes the governing rule of a true believer's heart. As a citizen of God's kingdom, a new allegiance to God's law begins. The authentic child of God will still periodically disobey God's Word, but not with the reckless abandon that characterizes the life of an unbeliever who practices lawlessness.

JESUS TOOK AWAY SINS

The reason a Christian will not practice lawlessness is because Christ came to this earth to die for our sins and break the power of sin in our lives.

> And you know that He appeared in order to take away sins; and in Him there is no sin. (1 John 3:5)

When Jesus died for our sins, He delivered us from the penalty, power, and practice of sin. The penalty of sin has been paid in full and the power of sin has been broken. Sin no longer is the dominant force of our lives because Christ died to take away sins at the Cross. Sin's penalty is cancelled, sin's power is conquered; therefore, sin's practice is reversed.

When Christ appeared to take away our sins, He shouldered our sins Himself. The words *take away* mean "to remove something by lifting it up." It gives the image of a strong man lifting a very heavy object in order to carry it far away. This is exactly what took place at the Cross. Jesus bore our sins in His own body, completely taking the crushing weight of sin off of us. He took away the penalty of sin and broke the power of sin in a believer's life.

As a result, no one who abides in Christ will continue to practice the sin Jesus died to remove. To be saved is to be delivered *from* something as well as *for* something. In salvation, we are rescued from sin and hell and preserved for holiness and heaven. Contrary to popular thinking, Jesus came to save us *from* our sins, not in our sins (Matthews 1:21). If one could continue to practice sin after being saved from sin, it would make Christ's death ineffective. God forbid!

WE DIED WITH HIM

When Jesus died for our sins, we died with Him to sin. Sin is still alive within us, but we are no longer alive to sin. "He Himself bore our sins in his body on the cross, that we might die to sin and live to righteousness" (1 Peter 2:24). When Jesus died for our sins, we died to sin. The power of sin was broken at the cross. Sin, the cruel master who once governed our life, is now impeached from office and a new king is installed.

A great preacher of yesteryear, Robert G. Lee, took his first trip to the Holy Land and stood at Calvary. The tour guide asked, "How many of you have been here before?" Dr. Lee raised his hand.

Perplexed, the tour guide said, "I thought you said this was your first trip."

"Oh, no," Dr. Lee said, "I was here two thousand years ago."

That's right. When Jesus died, we died with Him. Paul is saying, we used to have a master whose name was sin, and he ruled over our lives. But through the Cross we have been released from this slavery and been delivered to a new Lord who now directs our lives. Because Christ is our Master, we no longer have to obey our old master, sin. All who receive Christ's pardon also receive His power—a conquering power to live victoriously over sin (1 Corinthians 10:13). The one who does not experience His power over sin does not have His pardon for sin. Plain and simple.

THE BELIEVER'S UNION WITH CHRIST

John tells us that Christ who died for us lives within us. Our union with Him enables us to live victoriously over sin.

> No one who abides in Him sins; no one who sins has seen Him or knows Him. Little children, make sure no one deceive you; the one who practices righteousness is righteous, just as He is righteous. (1 John 3:6–7)

No one who abides in Him, John says, will practice sin as an ongoing lifestyle. This does not mean that we never commit sin, but that we can never *practice* sin again as we once did. When Jesus Christ takes up His royal residence in us, He will not tolerate the unbroken practice of sin within us. Because we live in continual union with Him who has no sin (3:5), we can no longer be habitual sinners in thought, word, or deed. We have the new desire to pursue righteousness and the indwelling Christ empowers us in this pursuit.

"The one who practices righteousness," referring to a lifestyle of holiness, is the one who "is righteous." A true believer has both a right standing before God and practices a right life before God. The difference between practicing righteousness and being righteous is the difference between justification and sanctification.

Being righteous refers to justification; practicing righteousness refers to sanctification. Justification instantly imputes the righteousness of Christ to the believing sinner, resulting in a right standing before God. Sanctification is the lifelong process by which the one who believes in Christ is brought progressively into conformity with the practical righteousness of Jesus Christ. Justification is positional; sanctification is practical. Justification is immediate; sanctification is progressive.

Whoever is justified is also being sanctified—it's a package deal. The apostle Paul says, "But by His doing you are in Christ Jesus, who became to us wisdom from God, and righteousness and sanctification, and redemption" (1 Corinthians 1:30). All four of these spiritual riches become ours at the moment of salvation. When Christ's redemption became ours, so did His wisdom, righteousness, and sanctification. When the perfect righteousness of Christ became ours at our conversion to Christ, so also did His sanctification. These two works of grace cannot be separated. "The one who practices righteousness" (sanctification) is the one who "is righteous just as He is righteous" (justification).

VICTORY IN JESUS

John goes a step further and provides another reason why a genuine Christian cannot practice sin. It is because Christ came to destroy the works of the devil, delivering those who are in bondage to sin.

> The one who practices sin is of the devil; for the devil has sinned from the beginning. The Son of God appeared for this purpose, to destroy the works of the devil. (1 John 3:8)

The devil, the greatest sinner of all, holds all unbelievers in his power (1 John 5:19). How powerful is Satan's control over an unbeliever?

First, Satan darkens their minds. Scripture says, "the god of this world has blinded the minds of the unbelieving so that they might not see the light of the gospel of the glory of Christ, who is the image of God" (2 Corinthians 4:4). Second, he defiles their hearts. Of all unbelievers Jesus said, "You are of your father the devil.... He was a murderer from the beginning, and does not stand in the truth because there is no truth in him. Whenever he speaks a lie, he speaks from his own nature, for he is a liar and the father of lies" (John 8:44). Third, he deadens their wills. "And you were dead in your trespasses and sins, in which you formerly walked according to the course of this world, according to the prince of the power of the air, of the spirit that is now working in the sons of disobedience" (Ephesians 2:1–2). Satan dominates all unbelievers so that they will ever live in open rebellion to God.

But Jesus Christ came to crush the power of the devil. At the cross our Lord won a great victory over the powers of darkness. Through His death, Jesus Christ utterly destroyed the works of the devil so that He might release us from Satan's evil empire. In so doing, Jesus broke the stronghold Satan once had over our lives.

Because Christ conquered Satan, a true believer will no longer habitually practice sin. Jesus' victory released all who believe in Him from Satan's tyranny, setting them free to never practice sin again—never! Emphatically, Jesus stated, "Everyone who commits sin is the slave of sin.... So if the Son makes you free, you will be free indeed" (John 8:34, 36). It is inconceivable that those who have been rescued from Satan's stronghold would continue practicing the very sin Jesus delivered them from.

A NEW NATURE OF HOLINESS

In addition, a genuine Christian cannot practice sin because he receives a new nature from God. This new, holy disposition desires to obey and please God.

> No one who is born of God practices sin, because His seed abides in him; and he cannot sin, because he is born of God. (1 John 3:9)

"The seed" is a metaphor for the new life of Jesus Christ planted within us that produces the fruit of a righteous life. When we are born of God, He plants His seed within us, which is a holy nature like His own. The new birth causes a dramatic, radical change within us. We become a new creation in Christ. Old things pass away, and new things come (2 Corinthians 5:17). This divine seed gives birth to a new life that forsakes our old pattern of sin and pursues a new path of holiness.

Martyn Lloyd-Jones writes, "Regeneration is the implanting of new life in the soul. It is the act of God by which a principle of new life is implanted in a man or woman with the result that the governing disposition of the soul is made holy." The fundamental disposition of our old sinful self is replaced by the Holy Spirit as He plants His holy nature in our soul. This new nature now determines how I behave and live. When God's holy seed is planted, a holy life blossoms.

No longer can we practice sin because it is inconsistent with the new seed within us. Just as a seed planted in the ground produces a new life that is consistent with its kernel, so God's seed—His divine nature—planted within us produces a righteous life. Like produces like! Apple seeds produce apples, and God's righteous seed produces righteousness. Regeneration is the root, righteousness the fruit. But no fruit? No root.

A CHANGE YOU CAN SEE

This change is very noticeable. Who is a child of God, and who is not, becomes very clear.

> By this the children of God and the children of the devil are obvious: anyone who does not practice righteousness is not of God, nor the one who does not love his brother. (1 John 3:10)

The obvious difference between the children of God and the children of the devil is this: the true believer practices righteousness; the unconverted person, whether church member or not, does not. You shall know them by their fruit, Jesus said (Matthew 7:16–20). A good tree will produce good fruit, a bad tree will produce bad fruit. A bad tree cannot produce good fruit. The fruit always reveals the kind of tree it is. So it is with the one who is born of God.

The moment we are regenerated, God does something in us that deposes the rule of sin in our lives and plants His divine seed within us. This seed germinates and produces a growing desire for holiness, righteousness, and love. Whenever God causes this change it becomes self-evident, leading to the assurance of one's salvation.

THE BIRTH OF CHANGE

Are you absolutely sure about your salvation? Then before the Lord, answer these questions honestly: Has there ever been a divine conception within you? Has God ever acted upon your dead soul and given you a new beginning? Have the old things ever passed away? Have new things come? Have you ever stopped practicing sin? Have you ever started practicing righteousness?

The answers to these questions will reveal whether or not you have been born again. As you see God at work within your life, producing these changes, He will confirm within you the assurance of your salvation. But if you do not see these virtues in your life, you need to reexamine whether you have truly believed in Christ.

You must see your sin that separates you from a holy God and declare personal bankruptcy before Him. Feel the guilt of your sin and confess it to God. Believe in Christ who shed His blood at the Cross, making the only provision for your sin.

Cast yourself upon Him now, and He will change you forever.

Chapter ten

THE LOVE
THAT INSPIRES HATE

Vital Sign #8: Conflict with the World

1 JOHN 3:11–13

Persecution is one of the surest signs
of the genuineness of our Christianity.

Benjamin E. Fernando

A soldier who was a Christian made it his practice to conclude every day with Bible reading and prayer. As his fellow soldiers gathered in the barrack and retired for the night, he would kneel by his bunk and offer prayers to the Lord.

The other soldiers saw this and began to mock and harass him. But one night the abuse went beyond verbal assault. As the soldier bowed before His Lord in prayer, one antagonist threw his boot through the dark and hit him in the face. The other soldiers snickered and jeered, hoping for a fight.

But there was no retaliation. The Christian soldier served a higher Commander in Chief who had issued orders to return evil with good.

The next morning when the taunting soldier awoke, he was startled to discover something at the foot of his bed. For all to see, there were his boots, returned and polished.

Rather than get even, the threatened soldier responded with the love of Christ. The irony is, it was his devotion for Christ that provoked the attack.

HATRED WITHOUT A CAUSE

Such persecution should not surprise us, for it mirrors the experience of the Lord Jesus Christ. No one ever loved more than Christ, yet no one was ever hated more than He.

Jesus reached out to all kinds of people, especially to those who had been passed over by this world. Extending kindness to the downtrodden, the riffraff, and the despised, Jesus poured out His compassion and grace upon the leftovers of this world. He was the friend of sinners (Luke 15:2). Yet the more He loved the unlovely, the more He was rejected by the self-righteous leaders of Israel.

Nowhere was this more evident than when Jesus healed a blind man on the Sabbath (John 9:1–7). Our Lord rubbed mud on the man's darkened eyes and told him to go wash in the pool of Siloam. When this man obeyed, instantly he was given sight, which provoked the wrath of the spiritual leaders because Jesus had done a good work on the Sabbath.

It was this expression of love, as well as other acts of kindness, such as raising Lazarus from the dead, that would ultimately lead to Jesus' crucifixion. Because He reached out with tender compassion to heal this blind man, our Lord was hated by the spiritual elite of Israel. Strangely enough, *the more He loved, the more He was hated.*

Even as He hung upon the cross, bearing the sins of the world, He was ridiculed, mocked, and blasphemed by those around Him. Never, I say never, was such love so hated.

FOLLOWING IN CHRIST'S STEPS

As we follow in Christ's footsteps, we too will provoke the antagonism of an unbelieving world. Jesus said, "'A slave is not greater than his master.' If they persecuted Me, they will also persecute you" (John 15:20). If we are to live like Christ, then we must suffer like Him. "All who desire to live godly in Christ Jesus will be persecuted" (2 Timothy 3:12).

The more we live as Christ lived, the more we will be rejected as

He was rejected. Unintentionally, our life will be irritating to this world, like salt rubbed into a raw, open wound. Our rejection of the world's godless values will provoke their hatred. Our stand for the truth will inspire their violent reaction as it clashes with their message of tolerance and moral relativity. And our love for the Lord provokes their anger because it is this allegiance to Him that instills His values and truth within us.

But blessing comes from buffeting. We may gain the assurance that our faith is real when we draw the opposition of unbelievers and suffer for our faith in Jesus Christ. If we are never rejected by the world, we have reason to question whether we have been accepted by Christ. And, by and large, if we are accepted by the world, we may conclude we are rejected by Christ. Only if we face persecution for His name can we know that we truly belong to Him.

THE MESSAGE NEVER CHANGES

As John begins this next section, he reminds us that the Christian message never changes. It is always the same.

> For this is the message which you have heard from the beginning, that we should love one another. (1 John 3:11)

John says his message is the same as the one they heard "from the beginning" of their Christian lives. The messenger may change, the methods may change, but the message remains the same. From the outset of their Christian walk, these early believers heard the very same message John now brings. Nothing has changed.

Why would John belabor this point? Because false teachers were coming into the church and altering the message. They were teaching things that were contrary to the sound doctrine the church had been taught from the beginning. In this verse John is saying, "Don't let anyone tell you anything that is new or different."

As I mentioned in an earlier chapter, these gnostic teachers had penetrated the church with their teaching, claiming that God was giving them special revelation. This spiritual elitism was dividing the church into the haves and the have-nots, or those who were supposedly receiving this mystical revelation from God and those who were not. The congregation was being splintered into carnal cliques and holy huddles made up of these super saints sharing their latest, falsely fabricated "God told me" updates. Those who claimed to be receiving these private revelations were soon looking down their noses at those who had "only" the Scriptures and the apostles' teaching.

Correction was in order by John.

LOVE ONE ANOTHER

The much-needed message for this congregation was not some new revelation. To the contrary, they needed to hear again the same old truth they had heard from the beginning—love one another. Love has been God's unchanging message from the outset. Next to loving God, the greatest commandment is our duty to love others (Matthew 22:37–40). Jesus said, "A new commandment I give to you, that you love one another, even as I have loved you" (John 13:34).

The apostle John reinforces this instruction and makes loving others nonnegotiable in the Christian life. We are to pay back every debt except the debt of love which is due others, an outstanding obligation that can never be repaid (Romans 13:8). Without love, everything we do, even our most spiritual activities, is worthless (1 Corinthians 13:1–3). Even when faith and hope pass away, love endures forever (13:13). In fact, love is the leading evidence of walking in the Spirit (Galatians 5:22).

This will never change. Love for Christ is primary in the Christian life (Revelation 2:4). And love for others is the visible expression of our love for Him (1 John 4:20–21).

Spiritual growth in Christ will always lead us to love others more. Christian maturity will never lead us into a reclusive selfishness that draws us away from others. Rather, the more we love God, the more we will love others. Real maturity will produce real love for real people.

But therein lies the problem.

WHEN IT KILLS TO LOVE

As we grow in our love for one another, such compassion, strangely enough, creates conflict. The more we love others in the world, the more we can expect to be persecuted by the world. In a note of sober warning, John continues:

> For this is the message which you have heard from the beginning, that we should love one another; not as Cain, who was of the evil one and slew his brother. And for what reason did he slay him? Because his deeds were evil, and his brother's were righteous. (1 John 3:11–12)

You will recall that Cain was the first child born to Adam and Eve (Genesis 4:1). Although he was a worshiper of God, he didn't love God and, therefore, his worship was not acceptable to God. Cain was religious but lost and went through the empty motions of worship because his heart was not right with God. Abel, the second born, loved God and his worship was approved by the Lord. As a result, Abel's love for God and his acceptance by the Lord provoked jealousy in Cain's heart, causing him to kill his brother. At the dawn of human history, this first persecution stands as a prototype of the ill treatment that would come to all believers who love God.

According to Genesis 4, Cain was a farmer and Abel a shepherd (4:1–2). Both sons were religious, both were worshipers (outwardly at least) of the one true God, both brought sacrifices to God, but one was refused, the other accepted.

According to the biblical account, Cain "brought an offering to the LORD of the fruit of the ground" while Abel "brought of the firstlings of his flock and of their fat portions" (4:3–4). As a result, "the LORD had regard for Abel and for his offering; but for Cain and for his offering He had no regard" (4:4–5).

Why were Cain and his offering refused by God but Abel and his offering received? Although this passage does not spell out a clear reason, some observations are worth noting. Both Cain and his offering were rejected. In other words, something was wrong with Cain when he came to worship, and something was wrong with his offering. Both the offerer and the offering were unacceptable to God.

UNACCEPTABLE WORSHIP

Let's begin with Cain himself. He was unacceptable to God because his heart was not right. That much is obvious from his angry response (4:5). Worship that pleases God must come from a pure heart. The wicked heart that lay behind his sacrifice was full of pride, hatred, and hypocrisy rather than humility, love, and sincerity. No wonder God refused him!

Moreover, Cain's offering was wrong. Though not specifically recorded in this passage, we can conclude that a blood sacrifice was required as an offering for his sin. This is implied from Genesis 3 when God Himself slew an animal to make coverings for Adam and Eve following their sin. In the killing of an animal, one life was given for another—a foreshadowing of future blood sacrifices required by God to cover sin.

But Cain approached God without a blood sacrifice. He brought what he wanted to bring, some of his crop, rather than a blood sacrifice as instituted by God. As a result, Cain's self-styled religion was rejected by God. So God had no respect for Cain nor any regard for his offering. Both his heart and his offering were wrong before the Lord and both were refused.

Abel, on the other hand, came before God in worship in an acceptable fashion and was received by the Lord. His heart was right, and his offering was right. He brought an animal, a blood sacrifice, the very best of the flock—of the firstlings of his flock. Later, Scripture tells us, "without shedding of blood there is no forgiveness" (Hebrews 9:22). From the very beginning, God had instituted blood sacrifices as the only pleasing offering for sin a worshiper could bring. Abel obeyed the Lord; Cain did not. Abel was accepted by the Lord; Cain was not.

As a result, "Cain became very angry and his countenance fell" (Genesis 4:5). Rather than repent, this older brother, an unbeliever and a false worshiper, became enraged at God. One could see the anger written on his face.

"Then the LORD said to Cain, 'Why are you angry?'" (4:6). God diagnosed something terribly wrong with Cain's heart as he came to worship—anger stemming from an unbelieving heart. The heart of his problem was the problem of his heart. God knew why Cain was upset, but He asked this question to force Cain to search his heart.

In so many words, God said, "If you had come with the right heart and the right offering, I would have accepted your worship. But your problem is sin within your heart, crouching like a lion ready to devour and destroy you. You must repent and overcome the sin in your heart" (4:7). Needless to say, he needed the right sacrifice to cover his sin— a blood sacrifice.

Did God's instruction bring Cain to repentance? On the contrary, God's Word only hardened his heart further. He refused God's call to forsake his sinful pride. And what was the result?

PERSECUTION ARISING FROM UNBELIEF

Now in open defiance, "Cain rose up against Abel his brother and killed him" (4:8). Why did this murder, the first act of violence in the history of the human race, occur? It was the result of Cain's anger toward God provoked by jealousy toward his brother. Being "of the evil one" (1 John 3:12), Satan filled Cain's heart to commit this murder. Rather than bring blood, he shed blood.

The apostle John explains that Cain killed Abel "because his deeds were evil, and his brother's were righteous" (1 John 3:12). Abel's life so convicted Cain that he killed Abel in an attempt to pacify the haunting convictions he felt.

Here is the first act of religious persecution by the world against a true believer, not by an atheist or an agnostic but by a false believer. Throughout the centuries, this scene would be repeated again and again, in both Old and New Testament alike, down to this very hour. Opposition and hatred will arise from an unbelieving world against true worshipers of God. Many times this persecution will arise within the church and come from counterfeit Christians, as represented in Cain, against true believers, as represented by Abel. At other times the persecution will come from those outside the church. But either way, the world will rise up to oppose true believers. And it will be this way to the very end.

IT'S TO BE EXPECTED

John now makes the obvious application to our lives. Persecution is to be expected from the world. The apostle succinctly concludes:

> Do not be surprised, brethren, if the world hates you. (1 John 3:13)

Make no mistake about it, the world of unbelievers will hate and oppose us, perhaps even kill us. Don't be surprised when it happens, John says. It's to be expected. The world will hate us. Even false believers within the Church, those who are religious but lost, will rise up against true believers.

It's been this way from the beginning of time. At the dawn of creation, Lucifer, a worshiper of God, incited many of his fellow worshipers among the angelic host to rebel against the Lord. As a result, they were banned from heaven and banished to the earth where, as Satan and his demonic hordes, they continue this rebellion by inciting conflict against true believers. A major part of Satan's strategy is to lead false worshipers of God, who masquerade as Christians, to persecute genuine believers.

So do not marvel when it happens, John writes. Every true worshiper of God can expect to face opposition. Unconverted worshipers infected with religious zeal, will always rise up to attack true believers.

JESUS RECEIVED IT!

This is precisely what happened to our Lord. It was the most religious people of Jesus' day, hardened and unconverted, who most hated Him and called for His crucifixion. In the case of our Lord, it was the false worshipers—the Pharisees, Sadducees, scribes, and the multitudes they led—who, like Cain, rose up and killed the one true lover of the Father, Jesus Christ.

It was the religious crowd of Jesus' day that persecuted Him. And it was primarily a religious crowd that first persecuted the apostles and the early church. Only later did the hatred come from the pagan nonreligious world of the Roman Empire and beyond. And it will be a religious crowd that will lead the persecution against us today as well.

Jesus said, "If the world hates you, you know that it has hated Me before it hated you. If you were of the world, the world would love its own; but because you are not of the world, but I chose you out of the world, because of this the world hates you" (John 15:18–19).

Nothing has changed over the years. Cain and Abel were both worshipers from the same family, attending, as it were, the same worship service. They were brothers, closely connected in their common pursuit to worship the one true God. But one was a counterfeit believer, the other was authentic. And the false believer rose up to kill the true one.

So it will be for you and me. The tares will always try to choke out the wheat. The goats will always attack the sheep. The Judases will always betray the followers of Jesus. The false converts will hate the true.

BLESSED ASSURANCE, PERSECUTION IS MINE

It is this persecution from the world that serves to strengthen the assurance of our salvation. Jesus says, "Blessed are you when men cast insults at you, and persecute you, and say all kinds of evil against you falsely, on account of Me" (Matthew 5:11). God's favor rests upon the one who suffers for Him. All true believers who live godly lives in Christ will receive, in one form or another, persecution and opposition. Though it is painful and hurts deeply, God always uses it for our good, and one primary good it brings us is the assurance of our salvation. Persecution clarifies for us whose side we are on. Suffering for Christ confirms to our hearts that we truly belong to Him. So as you are attacked for your faith in Christ, drawing the fire of opposition directed toward Christ, you can have a firm confidence that your faith in Christ is real. Jesus says to you, "Rejoice and be glad, for your reward in heaven is great; for in the same way they persecuted the prophets who were before you" (Matthew 5:12).

I have seen this to be true in my own life and ministry. As a preacher of the gospel and teacher of God's Word I have faced persecution, but none more furious than what has arisen from religious people within the church. The Word of God, a sharp, two-edged sword, cuts deeply into hearts. For those without Christ, it has led them either to be converted or to rise up in opposition against me. However, it is not I they sought to reject, but God.

You too will receive opposition from the world for your faith, even from among fellow worshipers. But rejoice, this opposition serves to bring the assurance of your salvation, a prized treasure.

BLESSING THROUGH BUFFETING

Examine your life. Have you suffered rejection because of your faith in Jesus Christ? Have you experienced animosity, hostility, or alienation from unbelievers because God is real in your life? Have you felt ostracism, prejudice, or hatred because you have represented Christ?

If so, then rejoice. This persecution of your faith validates the authenticity of your faith and brings the sweet assurance of your salvation. It is an indication that you belong to Him who suffered the same way for you.

SEPARATING THE TRUE FROM THE FALSE

Years ago a group of believers in Soviet Russia were meeting behind closed doors during the Communist regime's reign of terror. They huddled together in an obscure warehouse to worship the Lord, they fearing for their lives.

The worship service was in progress when their worst nightmare came to pass. The back doors of the rustic warehouse were suddenly thrown open and in walked four heavily armed Russian soldiers.

Down the center aisle of the church they marched, making their way to the front, where the leader said, "It is against the law to meet in worship except in the state-sanctioned church."

As his eyes scanned the tiny congregation, he said, "I will give you one chance to renounce your faith in Jesus Christ. If you will leave now and never return, I will forget I ever saw you here."

With mounting fear, the congregation began to disperse one by one until only the pastor and a handful of courageous souls remained. The commanding officer then ordered the back door bolted shut.

The pastor stepped forward and with trembling voice said, "Go ahead and shoot us, but we will not deny our Lord. He loved us unto death. We are ready to die for Him."

With that, the soldiers raised their rifles, only to lay them down. The officer then looked into the eyes of the pastor and said, "We too are believers in Jesus Christ. And we have come to worship with you. But we want to worship with *true* believers. We had to make this threat to find the real church. It would cost us our lives to worship with mere pretenders."

This persecution, though staged, served to identify the true worshipers of Jesus Christ. There was no doubt for these soldiers, nor for those who remained, who genuinely believed in Him who had died for them. Their persecution for Christ documented their faith in Christ.

BACKDOOR BLESSING

Let us be clear, persecution is to be expected from the world. But it is a backdoor blessing. The attack of the world is used by God to bring a settled confidence to our hearts that we are truly converted to Christ.

Until we suffer for our faith, it will remain suspect. But when opposition comes and we remain true to our convictions about Christ, it authenticates that our trust in Him is real.

The faith that is persecuted is the faith that is proven. But the faith that cannot be tested cannot be trusted.

Chapter eleven

PRIVILEGED

ACCESS

Vital Sign #9: Confidence in Prayer

1 JOHN 3:19–24; 5:14–15

We talk about heaven being so far away.
It is within speaking distance to those who belong there.

D. L. Moody

former king of Saudi Arabia, Abdul Aziz, passed a landmark decree in 1952 that provided every citizen of his country with the right of access to his throne. Every subject, he stated, had the right to come before him to present his petitions of complaint or requests for help. Even the poorest Saudi could approach his sovereign to plead his case. No countryman could be prohibited from coming.

Explaining this custom of privileged access, Crown Prince Fahd said, "Anyone, anyone can come here. That gives them confidence in their government.... They know they may look to us for help."

Think about this remarkable law. Here is a kingdom that grants every citizen, no matter who they are, the right to appear before their king.

But as incredible as this access is, it pales to insignificance when compared with the extraordinary privilege that belongs to every citizen of God's kingdom to approach His throne day or night. Every Christian has the right to approach an even greater monarch, the King of kings and Lord of lords, and look to Him for help.

ASSURANCE THROUGH PRAYER

We now approach the ninth and final vital sign that brings the assurance of salvation. It is very simply this: Do you live your life in reliance upon God in prayer? Do you approach God's throne regularly and bring your requests for help? All true citizens of heaven's kingdom will present themselves before their King to seek His support.

Moreover, do you see your prayers answered? God promises to answer the prayers of His children while refusing to hear the petitions of the wicked. One of the strongest proofs for the genuineness of our faith is that we see our prayers being answered. If God is your Father, you will ask and He will provide.

The Christian life cannot be explained apart from the supernatural presence and power of God. There is an incomprehensible dimension about every believer's life that goes beyond natural explanation. God Himself becomes the only possible explanation. In large part, this dynamic difference is explained by the privileged access of prayer that links us with almighty God in heaven. It is our confidence in prayer as we approach God's throne, as well as the answers to our prayers, that grants a settled confidence that we truly belong to Him.

BELONGING TO THE TRUTH

John begins his discussion of this last vital sign by affirming the God-given confidence every true believer has within his heart when he prays. The apostle writes:

> We will know by this that we are of the truth, and will assure our heart before Him. (1 John 3:19)

First, the apostle gives a vivid description of the one who is truly saved when he says "we are of the truth." Contrary to the testimony of many today, genuine believers are not portrayed as being "of their feelings" nor "of their emotions," but rather "of the truth."

We might say that for the Christian, the facts of the gospel are like the engine of a train, faith is the boxcar, and feelings the caboose. The order of these—facts, faith, feelings—is very important. It is our faith in the facts of the gospel that saves us, not our feelings toward the gospel. Our faith must pull our feelings, as an engine pulls a caboose, if we are to have an authentic assurance.

The one who is "of the truth" genuinely believes the truth of the good news of Jesus Christ and, as a result, is gripped, governed, and guided by the truth. This person's life is now controlled by the authority of God's Word.

Of such a person, John says, the truth assures his heart before God. That is to say, as a person is gripped by the truth of God's Word, the Holy Spirit provides assurance as one stands before God. To assume a position "before Him" is a reference to prayer in which we come by faith to stand before Him in humble dependence. Thus, we may have confidence before God in prayer, which, in turn, intensifies the assurance of our salvation.

CONFIDENCE BUILDER

Second, John states that we can "know...we are of the truth." That is to say, we can have the full assurance of our salvation. We can have the firm and settled confidence that we are genuinely bound for heaven long before we arrive there.

Reiterating what has been the constant theme of 1 John, the apostle states that the heart of the one who is "of the truth" shall assure him of his right relationship before God. This assurance, a full confidence within our hearts that we are truly saved, is produced by the Holy Spirit who lives within us as He continues to keep our faith in Christ active and strong.

GOD IS GREATER

Nevertheless, there are times when our heart is convicted before God, causing even a true child of God to be plagued with doubts. To this, John responds:

> In whatever our heart condemns us; for God is greater than
> our heart and knows all things. (1 John 3:20)

As believers, our own heart will often convict us of sin and, depending upon the severity of the inward condemnation, we may doubt the reality of our salvation. Fortunately, in such cases God remains greater than our heart. He alone knows whether or not we are saved. If we are genuinely converted to Christ, though we may be temporarily overcome with doubt, God knows the genuineness of our faith, even when we are unsure. When we look at our own lives honestly, we all see failure and sin. If we take seriously the message of 1 John, we will feel our hearts condemn us, causing us to search our own hearts and ask, "Am I truly saved?"

It is only natural for our hearts to condemn us as the perfect standard of God's Word is self-applied. As we look to isolated incidents in our lives rather than surveying the big picture, we will surely feel convicted and may even question our salvation. But in the heart of the one who is truly saved, the indwelling Holy Spirit brings the needed reassurance that we do belong to God. When we feel condemned, the Holy Spirit reaffirms that we really are a child of God if, in fact, He indwells us.

CONFIDENCE BEFORE GOD

If our heart does initially condemn us, God will provide the assurance we need to override our convicted heart. The apostle writes:

> Beloved, if our heart does not condemn us, we have confidence before God. (1 John 3:21)

The clear implication is, our hearts will condemn us. We will feel accused by our own conscience. But through this soul-searching process, our heart will be eventually reconfirmed and reestablished before God. We will soon have our confidence before God restored because He has brought true assurance, even reassurance, that we belong to Him. Confidence before God is not something we can generate; it is the work of the Holy Spirit who lives within us. "We know by this that He abides in us, by the Spirit whom He has given us" (3:24). Only God Himself can grant true assurance.

No pastor can give another person the confidence of his or her salvation. No parent, no counselor, no friend can give full assurance of one's salvation. Whatever someone else can talk you into, you can talk yourself out of. God, and God alone, can assure our hearts that we are genuinely saved.

Do you lack the assurance of your salvation? In your heart, do you doubt your relationship with God? If you have the Holy Spirit living within you, as all true believers do, He will restore your assurance— an assurance only He can bring.

SEEING GOD AT WORK

Specifically, what does the Holy Spirit use to reassure our hearts before God? One criteria for replenishing this assurance is seeing our prayers answered. We can know that God is in us when we see Him at work in our lives, answering prayers.

> And whatever we ask we receive from Him, because we keep
> His commandments and do the things that are pleasing in His
> sight. (1 John 3:22)

Notice the cause and effect here. We ask; God answers. If we are truly His children, God will answer our prayers because He hears the prayers of His children. It's that simple. The Holy Spirit within us will guide our prayers into the very center of God's will. As a result, our prayers will be predominantly on target with the desires of God because of the Spirit's intercession within us.

What if I am not genuinely saved? Then God will not answer my prayers. He will answer our prayers only in the name of Jesus (John 14:13–14), which requires that we have believed in Him.

In whatever we ask, we receive from Him. Nothing is too hard for God, nothing is impossible for Him. Whatever it is, if it is according to His will, He will answer. This privilege is open to all believers, not merely to a select few. So often we go without simply because we do not ask God to meet our needs. "You do not have because you do not ask" (James 4:2).

In response to our prayers, God activates His goodness, wisdom, and power to give us exactly what we need to carry out His will. Again, when we ask, we receive, all in His perfect timing, according to His perfect will. Let us remember, He is more eager to answer our prayers than we are to ask. He would do so much more than we can even imagine if we would just ask Him. When we do, we see God at work in our lives.

OBEDIENCE IS KEY

But there are conditions we are responsible to meet in prayer. God doesn't answer our every whim or lark. There are some prerequisites we must meet if we are to be in alignment with His will. God only answers our prayers as they are directed by the Holy Spirit into His will.

That's why obedience is so critically important if we are to see our prayers answered. We must be living in obedience to His Word if we are to be praying according to His will. As our lives are being brought into alignment with His character, His plan, and His purposes through obedience, God is pleased to answer our prayers.

FIRST THINGS FIRST

What commandments must we keep if we are to see our prayers answered? John lists two—one directed toward God, the other toward man.

> This is His commandment, that we believe in the name of His Son Jesus Christ, and love one another, just as He commanded us. (1 John 3:23)

If our prayers are to be answered, we must first obey the gospel and exercise personal, saving faith in Christ. The gospel is not a suggestion to consider nor an option to weigh but a commandment to obey. God commands all men everywhere to repent and believe the gospel (Acts 17:30). Conversely, unbelief is deliberate, defiant disobedience to the Word of God. Many people pray to God but don't even know the God to whom they pray. God is under no obligation to answer such prayers. He doesn't hear such prayers, not in the sense of giving a favorable response. There's only one way to come to God and that is through faith in Jesus Christ. Our Lord said, "I am the way, and the truth, and the life; no one comes to the Father but through Me" (John 14:6). Without a personal relationship with Christ, we have no basis whatsoever to come into God's holy presence. Until we believe in His name, we cannot pray in His name.

From this we may conclude we are rightly related to God in heaven through Jesus Christ as we see our prayers answered. We may know that we have truly believed in His Son as we receive from His hand.

But there is more.

THE COMMAND TO LOVE

There is a second commandment we must obey if our prayers are to be answered. That is the divine command to love one another. The two greatest commandments are that we love God supremely and love others sacrificially (Matthew 22:37–39). If we obey the first, we will obey the second. If we love God, we will love others. That's what John is saying here.

Loving others is a necessary prerequisite to having our prayers answered. First Peter 3:7 says if husbands do not love their wives as they should, their prayers will be hindered, meaning unanswered. Likewise, Jesus said if we do not forgive others, God will not hear us when we pray (Matthew 6:12–15). Thus, we must love others, caring for and forgiving them, if our prayers are to prevail with God.

Just as with believing the gospel, loving others is a commandment to obey, not a warm fuzzy feeling to follow. We are to love others even when the emotions are not there. In fact, the greatest love is when we reach out to help someone we have little feeling for. Anyone can love someone with whom he feels a camaraderie or connection. Jesus said even lost pagans love those who love them (Matthew 5:46–47). The challenge is to love someone who is difficult to love.

But love others we must. We are commanded to love because it glorifies God and spreads His goodness abroad on the earth. Such unconditional love aligns us with the heart of God and positions us to pray for what is God's will. As we love others, our hearts are aligned with God's will. And as our hearts are so directed, our prayers are on target with God's will, leading to the granting of our requests. This in turn increases assurance in our hearts that we are children of God.

ABIDING IN CHRIST

The apostle John wraps up this section with a final word about God-given assurance. Again, the context is prayer:

> The one who keeps His commandments abides in Him, and He in him. We know by this that He abides in us, by the Spirit whom He has given us. (1 John 3:24)

The ones who obey God's commandments are those who know "He abides in us." Specifically, these commands are those mentioned in the previous verse, the command to believe in Christ and to love others. The one who exercises saving faith in Christ is ushered into a supernatural relationship with Him, one in which we abide in Him and He in us. We couldn't be any closer or intimate with Christ than this. When we abide in Him, God answers our prayers.

Jesus said, "If you abide in Me, and My words abide in you, ask whatever you wish, and it will be done for you" (John 15:7). When we are one with Christ and His Word, we are one with His will and eternal purposes. What He wants is then what we want, and our prayers prevail with God.

As we enjoy this abiding relationship with Christ, the Holy Spirit within us brings the assurance of our salvation to our hearts. We know that Christ lives within us by the Spirit's witness within us. "The Spirit Himself bears witness with our spirit that we are children of God" (Romans 8:16). The Holy Spirit confirms to our inner person the validity of our true, saving relationship with Christ. Such inner assurance can come only from God.

CONFIDENCE IN PRAYER

Before he concludes 1 John, the apostle returns to the subject of prayer and discusses again our confidence before God. When we come before God in prayer, we should have great confidence that He will hear us and answer according to His perfect will.

> This is the confidence which we have before Him, that, if we ask anything according to His will, He hears us. And if we know that He hears us in whatever we ask, we know that we have the requests which we have asked from Him. (1 John 5:14–15)

John says we should have absolute confidence that we belong to God as we see Him answer our prayers. Simply put, God hears the prayers of His children.

If God did not hear us and give us good things, we should question whether we truly belong to Him because He does hear his children and give them what they need. Jesus said if earthly fathers give what their children need, will not God our heavenly Father give to us, His spiritual children, what we ask? "What man is there among you who, when his son asks for a loaf, will give him a stone? Or if he asks for a fish, he will not give him a snake, will he? If you then, being evil, know how to give good gifts to your children, how much more will your Father who is in heaven give what is good to those who ask Him!" (Matthew 7:9–11).

The fact that God hears our prayers means that He listens with the intention to answer. He is always listening intently to our prayers. God is always waiting to hear from us, wanting us to come before His throne with our requests, and is eager to provide for our needs according to His will.

DRAWING NEAR

The Bible affirms, "Therefore let us draw near with confidence to the throne of grace, so that we may receive mercy and find grace to help in time of need" (Hebrews 4:16). Likewise, "We have confidence to enter the holy place by the blood of Jesus" (Hebrews 10:19). Because we have confidence to enter, we have confidence that He hears and will answer. God has not provided this access into His presence at the price of His Son's life *not* to hear us.

The apostle Paul reasoned, "He who did not spare His own Son, but delivered Him over for us all, how will He not also with Him freely give us all things?" (Romans 8:32). God, having given us the greatest gift, Jesus Christ, will surely give us the lesser gifts, meaning whatever is necessary to carry out His will.

As we come before Him, prayer is not a device for imposing our will upon God's will, but the means of submitting our will to His, and requesting whatever we need to do His will. Wherever God guides, God provides. It is by prayer that we seek God's will and subordinate ourselves to Him. Even as Jesus prayed, "Not My will, but Yours be done" (Luke 22:42), so must we pray, "Your kingdom come. Your will be done, on earth as it is in heaven" (Matthew 6:10).

An when we do humble ourselves before God's throne, He will move heaven and earth to carry out His will through us, His children.

GOD OF THE IMPOSSIBLE

Shortly after Dallas Theological Seminary opened its doors, the fledgling school stood on the brink of bankruptcy. So serious was the problem that all its creditors were going to foreclose on the institution on a particular day at noon.

Responding to the crisis of the hour, the school's founders met in President Lewis Sperry Chafer's office to pray that God would provide the resources they so desperately needed. In that prayer meeting was Harry Ironside, the noted pastor of Moody Memorial Church in downtown Chicago.

When it was Ironside's turn to pray, he poured out his heart. "Lord, we know that the cattle on a thousand hills are Thine. Please sell some of them and send us the money."

At the very time they were praying, a tall Texas rancher walked into the seminary's office and said something that dramatically altered the future of the school.

"I just sold two carloads of cattle in Fort Worth," the man explained to the receptionist. "I've been trying to make a business deal go through, but it won't work. I feel that God is compelling me to give this money to the seminary. I don't know if you need it or not, but here's the check."

A secretary took the check and, knowing something of the seriousness of the hour, went to the door of the prayer meeting and timidly tapped, not wanting to interrupt the session of prayer.

When she finally got a response, Dr. Chafer took the check from her and saw that it was for the exact amount of the debt. A smile came over his face. Then he looked at the signature and recognized the name of the cattle rancher.

Turning to Dr. Ironside, he said, "Harry, God sold His cattle."

Although not always answered so dramatically, God does hear our prayers and answers them as we pray according to His will. What confidence ought to fill our hearts as we approach His throne of grace. In the name of Christ, we have privileged access to enter His presence and receive the help we need to live victoriously in Christ.

GOD HEARS HIS CHILDREN

Thus, John lists answered prayer as the final means that leads to the assurance of our salvation. When we pray and God answers, this gives us great confidence that we really do have a genuine relationship with Him.

Does God hear you when you pray? Does God answer? Do you see the invisible hand of God at work in response to your prayers? Have you prayed for the salvation of an unbeliever, perhaps a family member or friend, and seen that person come to faith in Christ?

Have you sought God about a tremendous need in your life and seen Him meet it? Have you prayed for guidance and received it? Have you asked for peace in the midst of a trying circumstance and experienced it? Have you faced an impossible situation and seen God turn it around for you?

As you see God answer your prayers, be encouraged. He answers the prayers of His children. Answers to our prayers bring the confident assurance of our salvation.

EXAMINE YOURSELF

Are You in the Faith?

The worst ignorance in the world is not to know ourselves.

J. C. Ryle

God wants each of His children to know beyond a shadow of any doubt that he or she has eternal life. The apostle John writes, "These things I have written to you who believe in the name of the Son of God, so that you may know that you have eternal life" (1 John 5:13). God does not desire that we be uncertain about our eternal destiny; He wants us to be absolutely sure that salvation is ours.

We can be certain that our faith is real as we see the evidences of eternal life within us. The nine vital signs we've looked at in 1 John provide the basis for the blessed assurance every true believer longs to possess. We can have a settled confidence that heaven is our future home as we see God at work in our lives, conforming us into the image of Jesus Christ.

The Bible says, "Test yourselves to see if you are in the faith; examine yourselves!" Rather than looking to a past decision for Christ, let us look to a present reality deep within our souls. As we see our faith alive and active, bringing forth the fruit of righteousness, we can be absolutely sure.

BREAKING BREAD TOGETHER

Imagine you are attending a Sunday evening Communion service at a local church. As people enter the worship center, their hearts are solemn. Coming to the Lord's Table is always a special time in the life of any Christian, and tonight will be no different.

After a few hymns and choruses, the pastor steps to the pulpit and asks the people to begin to prepare their hearts for the Communion that will follow.

"We must always examine ourselves as we come to the Lord's Supper," he begins.

The pastor turns to 1 Corinthians 11 and reads verses 27 and 28: "'Whoever eats the bread or drinks the cup of the Lord in an unworthy manner, shall be guilty of the body and the blood of the Lord. But a man must examine himself, and in so doing he is to eat of the bread and drink of the cup.'

"As we approach the Lord's Supper, these verses call us to examine ourselves. Specifically, they call us to examine the genuineness of our profession of faith in Christ, whether we are in the faith or not. Not everyone who names the name of Christ is truly saved. With the need to search our hearts, then, let's turn to 1 John for God's examination checklist."

LOOKING TO GOD'S STANDARD

"We must make certain that our faith is a real, saving faith. That's why the book of 1 John is so valuable to us, because it gives us this checklist by which to take a spiritual inventory. It is so critical, you may want to write down these evidences of true salvation so you can best examine your own life."

The sound of rustling paper is heard all through the worship center as people scurry for notebook paper or the back of a bulletin.

"The new birth will always be accompanied by certain evidences that confirm that your salvation is real," the pastor continues. "*Vital signs,* we could call them. Feeling the pulse of these vital signs in your life gives assurance of your salvation. But if in the examination of your life you fail to see them, then you must know that your faith falls short of true, saving faith.

"Go ahead and number one through nine down the left-hand side of the page. I want you to record all nine of these vital signs of salvation. If you are to properly judge yourself, this is what you need to check in your life to have genuine assurance.

"Ask yourself these questions. If you can answer yes to these nine questions, then the assurance of salvation should be yours to enjoy."

VITAL SIGNS OF SAVING FAITH

"First, *do you desire communion with Christ?* An authentic child of God will enjoy fellowship with Christ. Religion is all external activity and outward ritual, but Christianity is intensely personal and internal. The one who believes in the Lord Jesus Christ truly knows Him. So, let me ask you, do you have a personal relationship with Jesus Christ?

"Second, *do you practice confession of sin?* A true believer is greatly aware of his or her sin and will acknowledge that sin to God. Do you confess your sin on a regular basis?

"Third, *do you have a deepening commitment to God's Word?* Every true believer has a hunger for God's Word. Jesus says in John 15:7–8, 'If you abide in Me, and My words abide in you...you bear much fruit, and so prove to be My disciples.' Let me say as pointedly as I can, all who have been born of God long to know and obey His Word. Do I long for the pure milk of the Word so that I will grow in my faith?

"Fourth, *do you have compassion for fellow believers?* Upon admittance into God's family, a believer has a newfound love for his spiritual brothers and sisters in Christ. No longer hating the righteous, the one who has been saved has a heart to serve other Christians. Do you love other believers?

"Fifth, *do you see a growing change of desires?* As Paul says in Romans 6, the Christian has a new way of life. The one who is truly converted begins to hate the things he once loved and to love the things he once hated. Do you hate sin and love righteousness?

"Sixth, *do you seek a greater comprehension of the truth?* When we are regenerated, the Holy Spirit gives us eyes to see and minds to understand truth. Am I seeking to be puffed up with knowledge or do I comprehend truth in order to better know and serve God?

"Seventh, *do you show increasing conformity to Christlikeness?* The true believer continues to grow in Christ. The way you know you have been saved is that you are being sanctified. All Christians pursue righteous behavior. Like a greyhound pursuing a rabbit, so a Christian chases after holiness of life. Do I pursue holiness or do I pursue sin?

"Eighth, *are you in conflict with the world?* The Christian in pursuit of personal holiness runs head on into the world. The light of the believer's life exposes the deeds of darkness and convicts unbelievers, which then creates tremendous tension. Does your life collide with the world or are you in harmony with it?

"Ninth, *do you have confidence in prayer?* A true Christian lives his life in reliance upon God. He prays to God to meet his needs. Do you find yourself casting your cares upon Him or relying upon yourself?

"All nine of these evidences will be present and growing, in one degree or another, in the life of the one who is born again. Only those who see God producing these virtues in their lives can be absolutely sure of their salvation."

A RENEWED ASSURANCE

Sitting in the congregation, a businessman named Jim hears the pastor describe these evidences of the new birth and asks himself, *Are these vital signs present in my life?*

As he inspects his own soul, the Holy Spirit turns the searchlight on and enables Jim to see himself as he truly is. Although he does not see these signs perfectly realized, they nevertheless are clearly the ongoing desire of his heart and direction of his life.

Jim sees God at work in his life. Yes, he enjoys fellowship with Christ that produces a deep sensitivity to sin and a growing desire to obey God's Word. When he does sin, he seeks to immediately confess it to God. At the same time, there is a deepening love for other believers, an increasing passion for God, and a growing disregard for the world. Because the Holy Spirit is within him, Jim's eyes are open to the truths of God's Word, and his life is being transformed into the image of God's Son, creating within him the righteous character of God. Furthermore, this changed life brings persecution from the world, which drives him even closer to God in confident prayer.

Stronger than any subjective, mystical feelings, these evidences of God's grace at work in Jim's life bring a deep assurance that he is a true child of God. More than any past religious experience he can look back to, this recognition of God's present work of grace in his life brings unspeakable joy. This is true assurance. Jesus is mine!

REPELLED BY THE TRUTH

Sitting on the other side of the worship center is a single girl named Jane. She too has been challenged to examine herself before she takes Communion, but tragically, as she looks within, something is missing. The same call to self-examination that caused Jim to rejoice causes her to reject what was said. The same sun that melts the ice hardens the clay. Even so, the same truth that brings confirmation to one person incites infuriation in another. The Word of God has so provoked Jane that she is unwilling to examine her heart any more. It's too painful for her.

How dare someone question my relationship with God, she fumes. *I grew up in this church. I was baptized in this church. I've been in the Christmas pageant for over ten years. Who does he think he is suggesting that I need to examine whether or not I am in the faith?*

The truth of the matter is, the evidences of saving grace are woefully absent in Jane's life. The same message that confirmed assurance in Jim is now condemning her. Smoldering on the inside, she grabs her Bible and storms out of the worship center before Communion is served— never to return.

Jane fulfills the very Word of 1 John 2:19. "They went out from us, but they were not really of us; for if they had been of us, they would have remained with us; but they went out, so that it would be shown that they all are not of us."

The fact that she leaves with such anger and bitterness gives strong evidence that she is religious but lost. She refuses to examine herself any further because of what is truly there—an unconverted heart. She is living a lie.

THE BREAD AND THE WINE

The pastor sees Jane stomp out and storm away. Disturbed by this display, he tries to gather himself and to turn his attention back to the Lord's Supper. As the service shifts now to partaking of the Lord's Table, the preacher turns to Matthew's Gospel and reads from the Upper Room account. "While they were eating, Jesus took some bread, and after a blessing, He broke it and gave it to the disciples, and said, 'Take, eat; this is My body.' And when He had taken a cup and given thanks, He gave it to them, saying, 'Drink from it, all of you; for this is My blood of the covenant, which is poured out for many for forgiveness of sins'" (Matthew 26:26–28).

After reading these verses, the pastor talks about Christ's death on the cross. There, lifted up to die, He bore our sins in His body and absorbed God's wrath for our sins. Jesus died in our place and shed His blood, providing the only salvation by which we can be saved. It is in the shedding of Christ's blood, he explains, that sinners are forgiven and cleansed of their sin. Only through the blood of Christ can rebels be reconciled to a holy God.

SORROW UNTO SALVATION

Under the searchlight of God's word, Jessica, a teenage girl, examines her heart for evidences of the new birth. As she looks within, the Holy Spirit illumines her wretched state as she has never seen it before. Under deep conviction of sin, she begins to understand that she, a sinner, is separated from a holy God. The Spirit presses to her heart that the vital signs from 1 John are not present in her life.

Jessica mourns that her sins nailed Christ to the cross. She begins to weep silently. She has attended church all her life, but has never sensed her need for a Savior until now. With a sense of her unworthiness, she calls out to the Lord to save her. Committing her life to the lordship of Christ, she embraces Him by faith and rejoices in God's unconditional love for her.

Sixteen years of sin are now lifted off Jessica's back, and at last the peace of God floods her heart. Immediately, God begins to work in this young woman's life. In this instant, she is dead to sin and alive to Christ. Jessica takes Communion for the first time as a true believer in the Lord.

WHICH ONE ARE YOU?

Three different people responded in three different ways to the truth of God's Word. One was *confirmed* by the truth, one was *condemned* by it, and one was *converted* by it.

Which response most closely mirrors your own? As you have read the pages of this book, is your heart confronted, condemned, or confirmed?

If you know Christ, I pray that the Holy Spirit will make you absolutely sure of your salvation. If you do not know Him, I pray that you will not harden your heart, but repent of your sin and genuinely believe in Christ.

Do it today.

Eternity is at stake!

Chapter thirteen

ALL THAT TRULY MATTERS

Saved or Lost?

By delay of repentance, sin strengthens, and the heart hardens.
The longer ice freezeth, the harder it is to be broken.

Thomas Watson

ow that we have carefully considered the vital signs from 1 John, two truths need to be reinforced in our hearts. First, *God desires that true assurance be our joyful possession if we have truly believed in Christ.* As we see these evidences of God's grace at work in our lives, we should rejoice with a deep confidence that we are heaven-bound. More than simply looking to a past event, such as walking an aisle or praying a prayer, God's full assurance comes from discovering His present work of grace in our lives. Ultimately, it is His sanctifying work within us that provides the greatest certainty that we belong to Christ. This firm assurance is surely a foretaste of glory divine!

POSSESSION, NOT PROFESSION

But, second, *if you do not see your life being changed into Christlikeness, you need to consider whether or not you genuinely belong to Him.* Perhaps the reason for your lack of joy is that salvation has not yet come to your life. If that is the case, then I urge you to come to Christ and be saved before you put this book down.

In the final analysis, the assurance of our salvation comes not from our confession of Jesus Christ. Our Lord Himself said, "Not everyone who says to Me, 'Lord, Lord,' will enter the kingdom of heaven" (Matthew 7:21). It is possible to profess to know Jesus and yet not have a saving relationship with Him. Only a life changed by the power of God, along with the Holy Spirit's inner witness, confirms that your confession of Christ is real.

If after examining your life you have no assurance that you are saved and bound for heaven when you die, then consider the following incident, which occurred in my ministry. What happened to this man could happen to you as well.

"I NEED TO TALK"

After a recent church service, a businessman in his thirties made a bee-line for the pulpit area where I stood, desperate to reach me first. As he introduced himself, the tears in his eyes and the raspy tone in his voice signaled that something was weighing heavily upon his troubled heart.

"I really need to talk with you, Pastor," he said with great earnestness.

"What's wrong?" I asked.

He was unable to answer. His fallen countenance told me that whatever it was, we needed to talk now. So we retired to my study.

"I don't know if I'm saved," he sobbed. "I need to know where I stand with God."

"When do you think you became a Christian?" I asked.

He walked me through a typical childhood "decision" story, fraught with vague uncertainties, followed by years of an unchanged life, eventually a broken marriage, and now haunting doubt.

I presented the gospel of Jesus Christ to him, explaining the eternal implications of the cross and what it means to truly believe in Jesus, then asked if he had ever genuinely committed his life to the Lord.

WRESTLING WITH GOD

He had the look of a man wrestling with God, and his head began shaking from side to side. This man was an active member of our congregation and very involved in our church's Bible studies, yet he was now being convicted by the Holy Spirit that he was spiritually lost and without Christ.

After reviewing for him the gospel of grace, I asked him if he wanted to pray and receive Christ. At first, he was fearful to do this, then after a while he was fearful not to. With earnest desperation, he prayed with me, pouring out his soul to God and casting himself upon Christ for salvation.

In that very moment, my pastor's office was transformed from an "emergency room" to a "delivery room." This desperate young businessman was born again by God. With childlike faith, he repented of his sins and entered the kingdom of God by surrendering his life to Jesus Christ. After years of sterile worship services, empty church activities, and vain religiosity, he had now come to the end of himself and was experiencing the beginning of true salvation.

Assurance began to flood his heart for the very first time. His soul had now found its rest in Christ. A firm and settled confidence was now his own. He was saved.

This can happen to you as well. If you sense your need to be saved, I urge you to believe in Christ this moment. Commit your life to Him. Turn from yourself and trust Him to be your Lord and Savior.

All that truly matters is whether or not you are saved. Those doubts about your relationship with God that have haunted you so long may now drive you to faith and assurance. When Christ comes into a heart, the clouds of doubt are broken up and the sunlight of the certainty of His magnificent love and acceptance come shining forth. Believe in Him now and you may be saved.

Are you saved or lost?

Be absolutely sure.

ANSWERING THE MOST ASKED QUESTIONS ABOUT ASSURANCE

Assurance puts the heart in heaven, and moves the feet to heaven.

C. H. Spurgeon

As a pastor for the past twenty years, I have had to answer many questions on a variety of subjects, but without a doubt the most frequently asked questions are about the assurance of salvation. Though I am often asked "How can I know God's will?" or "Who should I marry?" or "What job should I take?" the question I'm asked the most is "How can I know I'm saved?"

I'm sure many questions about assurance have surfaced as you've read this book. In this appendix, I want to raise and answer the questions I hear most often as I sit in my pastor's office and listen to those who wonder whether they are truly saved.

Perhaps you are troubled by some of these same questions. Or maybe you are a counselor or a friend trying to help someone else work through these questions. Then continue reading for some insights I trust will give you the answers you are seeking.

1. Can a genuine Christian doubt his or her salvation?

John wrote his first epistle so that all who believe in Christ might know that they have eternal life (1 John 5:13). This clearly implies that some of the Christians John was writing to did have doubts about their salvation. First John would never have been written had not some true believers been doubting their salvation.

Along this line, the writer of Hebrews exhorted his readers to "show the same diligence so as to realize the full assurance of hope" (6:11). If he desired them to possess the full assurance of salvation, they were obviously experiencing a *partial* assurance, wavering in some doubt. A distraught father once said to Jesus, "I do believe; help my unbelief" (Mark 9:24). True faith may have some doubt.

So just because someone doubts his or her salvation does not mean that person is not a true believer.

2. Who can give me the assurance of my salvation?

Only God can give the confidence of a right standing before Him. No pastor, counselor, or friend can do this. Only the Holy Spirit can confirm to a heart the assurance of salvation. This is an intensely personal matter between God and me.

But please understand, God may use another person to point someone struggling with this issue in the right direction. Spiritually minded people can be instrumental in helping others gain a more complete understanding of the gospel and all that God has provided in salvation. Nevertheless, genuine assurance must come ultimately from the Holy Spirit who indwells the believer.

3. Can a new Christian experience the assurance of salvation?

Implicit within all true, saving faith is an element of assurance. The Bible affirms, "Faith is the assurance of things hoped for, the conviction of things not seen" (Hebrews 11:1). Simply put, all genuine faith has assurance inherent within it.

Granted, assurance will grow and blossom over time. As faith develops and matures, so will assurance. An initial, embryonic confidence toward God, genuine and real, will eventually grow and mature into a full assurance as evidences of Christlikeness are produced in one's life.

Nevertheless, assurance of salvation can be enjoyed the moment one genuinely believes in Christ.

4. Must I know the exact time and place of my conversion in order to have assurance?

Not necessarily. Assurance never comes from looking to a past event, but to a present reality. More important than knowing a specific moment of conversion is having a current faith in Christ and experiencing a present work of grace in one's life.

Nowhere in Scripture does God require one to pinpoint the exact moment new life in Christ begins. Obviously, such a decisive conversion experience has been the testimony of many. It certainly was with the apostle Paul (Acts 9, 22, 26). But not all conversions will be such a dramatic "Damascus Road" experience.

Many factors, such as one's age, the experience of sin, temperament, and how the gospel was presented, affect the emotional impact of one's salvation experience. Depending upon these and other factors, one person may know the exact moment of his conversion while another will not. But both can be genuine.

5. If I am genuinely saved, why do I doubt my salvation?

Many factors can cause one to doubt his or her salvation. As pain is helpful to let us know that something is wrong with our health, so doubt *may* be helpful to reveal that something is wrong with our spiritual well-being. When a true believer experiences significant doubt, it probably is an indicator that a spiritual problem exists.

Sinful behavior can cause one to doubt. Feelings of guilt produce a troubled conscience and can cause a person to question the validity of his or her salvation. In addition, unconfessed sin only provokes this restless feeling of uncertainty about salvation. Temptation from the world, if it is not resisted, can cause one to burn with lust. When these forces are brought to bear upon an already fragile faith, doubt can emerge.

Also, some people doubt their salvation because of a poor understanding of God's Word. They fail to grasp the meaning of God's grace. Believing they are somehow responsible to do good works to maintain their acceptance with God, they strive to keep themselves saved, little realizing that the eternal life they have received lasts for eternity.

Finally, some Christians doubt their salvation if they experience a painful trial. The death of a spouse, a doctor's diagnosis of cancer, or a job layoff may cause them to doubt whether God loves them.

But we must remember, if we have saving faith that does not mean all life's storms will be removed; rather true faith gives us the resources to sail through those storms victoriously. Jesus, the Son of God, experienced tribulation in this world, and so will all God's sons and daughters (Romans 5:1–5; 8:18–39; James 1:2–4).

6. I prayed to receive Christ as a child. Can that be real?

Absolutely. On one occasion, Jesus called a child to Himself and said, "Unless you are converted and become like children, you will not enter the kingdom of heaven" (Matthew 18:3). We can surmise, who better to exercise childlike faith than a child? Later, Jesus said, "Let the children alone, and do not hinder them from coming to Me; for the kingdom of heaven belongs to such as these" (Matthew 19:14).

In conversion, children do not need to become like adults; adults need to become like children. Childlike qualities of simple trust and humble dependence are necessary for true conversion. Again, a childlike faith can best be exercised by a child.

7. Must I submit my life to Christ at the time of conversion?

The Bible makes no distinction between Jesus as Savior and Jesus as Lord. When I truly believe in Christ to be my Savior, I will also begin to submit to Him as my Lord. Coming to Jesus as Savior requires a surrender to His Lordship.

Too often I hear someone say, "I received Jesus as my Savior when

I was nine, but I didn't make Him Lord and begin living for Him until I was twenty-one." That is a false testimony. Saving faith occurs when I make a commitment to Christ that effects a change of life, including living for Christ. A life of obedience begins immediately.

Christ is not received in installments. One cannot receive one part of Christ, His Saviorhood, without receiving the other part, His Lordship. Scripture says, "Believe in the *Lord* Jesus" (Acts 16:31) if we are to be saved. And, "If you confess with your mouth Jesus as *Lord*…you will be saved" (Romans 10:9). The name Jesus means "Jehovah saves," emphasizing His Saviorhood, and Lord means "sovereign ruler," emphasizing His authority to rule over our lives. Salvation occurs when I believe in and receive the *Lord* Jesus.

Jesus stands at the door of the sinner's heart, seeking entrance. The Lord says, "Behold, I stand at the door and knock; if anyone hears My voice and opens the door, I will come in to him and will dine with him, and he with Me" (Revelation 3:20). If the person without Christ says, "*Jesus,* come into my life, but *Lord,* stay out," He cannot and will not come in. Salvation is an all or nothing response to Christ in which we receive Him as both Savior and Lord.

8. What if I still see sin in my life?

You *will* see sin in your life whether you are saved or lost. The question is, how do you respond to your sin? Are you grieved that your sin violates the holiness of God? The unsaved person will sin and not care. He will even gravitate toward sin with increasing practice and pleasure. But when the saved person sins, he will be convicted by it and loathe it. Conversion does not mean we can no longer sin, but that we can no longer sin and enjoy it.

Avoid too much self-examination. This can lead to morbid introspection, which can lead to despair and depression, and rob your soul of joy and assurance! No amount of sanctification has ever saved anyone. We are saved by the finished work of Christ, whose righteousness is imputed to us by faith. We must look beyond ourselves to God's work for us in the sacrifice of Christ.

9. What must I examine to confirm my salvation?

The means by which we can know we are saved is threefold. Each is critically important.

First, *personal faith in God's Son*. The gospel says I am a great sinner and Christ is a great Savior who died for my sins, was buried, and rose again from the dead. Enthroned at God's right hand, Jesus is alive and able to save all who call upon Him. Have you ever believed upon Christ to save you?

Second, *the internal witness of God's Spirit*. Upon believing in Christ, God's Spirit comes to reside within me permanently, and He testifies to my heart that I belong to Christ. "The Spirit Himself testifies with our spirit that we are children of God" (Romans 8:16; cf. 1 John 3:24; 4:13).

Third, *the external reality of a transformed life*. The fruit of Christlikeness will become evident in my life, as described in the book of 1 John.

All three of these criteria must line up in our life, and when they do, a blessed assurance may be ours. Consider the following illustration that pictures this three-fold confirmation.

A tiny fishing ship on the open sea was suddenly caught in a tremendous storm. She immediately sought safety in the nearby harbor, but huge protruding rocks guarded the port's entrance, and it was dark that night.

The ship's crew radioed the port, "Give us directions for safe passage."

The reply came back, "Line up the three lights of the lighthouse, the church on the hill, and the moon. Then proceed with confidence full speed ahead."

As I believe in Christ, receive the Spirit's witness, and perceive a transformed life, I can have the true assurance that I am saved. Line up these three lights, then proceed with confidence!

10. Is there anything else that can help me determine whether or not I am saved?

Jesus once told a story about a sower of seed. As I recount that story, I invite you to find yourself in it and you will know whether you are saved or lost.

Jesus said a sower went out to sow seed and it fell upon four types of soil (Matthew 13:1-2). The first seed landed on the side of the road where the soil was hard and packed down, and the birds quickly devoured it before it could grow. The second seed fell on rocky soil, and though it initially sprang up, it soon died because the soil had no depth. The third seed fell among thorns and was choked out. The fourth seed fell upon good soil, fertile and prepared, and only it yielded a harvest.

Explaining this parable, Jesus said that the seed is the Word of God, the sower is the Son of God, and the different soils are the hearts of men. When the Word was sown into the first heart, it was hardened and not receptive to the Word and Satan, like a foul bird, snatched it up before it could grow. This person, although hearing the Word, disregarded the truth of the gospel and remained lost.

When the Word fell upon the second heart, there was an initial response, but it soon withered and died. The problem was a shallow heart. The roots had no depth because of a rocky ledge beneath the soil, and its growth was aborted. This heart, despite an apparent interest, had no real repentance from sin, no firm commitment to Christ, no genuine faith in the gospel. This person also is lost.

In the third heart, the thorns, representing the cares of the world, choked out the Word. The love of possessions, prestige, and popularity prevent God's Word from germinating and growing. This person also is lost. Love for God never supersedes love for the world.

Finally, in the fourth heart, God's Word grows and bears fruit. The soil has been plowed and made receptive to the seed. This soil is fertile and the seed germinates and produces a bumper crop. This life, and this life only, is saved. It alone produces fruit unto eternal life.

Which soil represents your life?

Has the Word been plucked from your heart? Or has there been an initial burst of interest in Christ, only to fizzle out, bearing no fruit? Or have the things of the world choked out your desire for spiritual things, again bearing no fruit? If so, then you are lost and need to be saved.

But if your life is marked by brokenness over sin, humble receptivity of God's Word by faith marked by obedience, and bearing the fruit of Christlikeness, then you are genuinely converted to Him.

Only God's Word working by God's Spirit can reveal where you stand regarding God's kingdom.